CHANGE
YOUR
BUSINESS

Christina L. Martini and David G. Susler

PARADIGM SHIFT

Part of the Paradigm Shift Series

CHANGE YOUR BUSINESS

ISBN 978-1-961185-82-1 (Paperback)
ISBN 978-1-961185-83-8 (Hardcover)
ISBN 978-1-961185-84-5 (eBook)

Cover Design, Book Formatting & Layout by *in omnia paratus publishing llc*

www.inomniaparatuspublishing.com

We are forever grateful to so many people for the professionals and individuals we are today. None of this would have been possible without the love, support, coaching and advice that we have received over the years.

We dedicate *Change Your Business* to our family, friends, colleagues, clients, mentors, coaches, confidantes, professors, teachers, role models and others who have so generously touched our lives and left their indelible imprints on us.

You know who you are.

TABLE OF CONTENTS

PREFACE

Nothing happens until something moves.
- Albert Einstein

A paradigm shift is defined as a fundamental change in how we think about or do something that leads to a new and different understanding or approach to a situation. This change often involves a significant shift in our beliefs, practices and perspectives, and can be inspired by the introduction of new knowledge or evidence.

As a practicing attorney with over 30 years of professional experience in BigLaw across a wide variety of practice areas, I have had countless opportunities to work with a wide range of clients on bet the company legal matters. These experiences inspired me over two decades ago to start sharing my professional and personal insights through various thought leadership, including my podcast (aptly named Paradigm Shift), as well as through dozens of columns, many written in tandem with my husband, who is also a lawyer and brings his own perspective and professional experiences.

This year, as I considered the many topics I have written about for over 20 years, I quickly realized that most, if not all, of them carry even more value now than at the time I had originally written about them, not only for my fellow legal professionals for whom they were originally written, but for everyone else. And, just like that, the idea for this book and our other book, *Change Yourself*, was born. Both books are intended to complement one another, and while they each have some of the same content, *Change Yourself* is focused on individuals and *Change Your Business* is targeted to organizations.

As I reflect on my legal career, and the professional and personal life I have created, I feel nothing short of blessed – blessed to have the family, friends, clients and colleagues, without whom none of this would have been possible, and blessed for the serendipities and opportunities which have crossed my path and transformed my journey of incredibly hard work and dedication to one which has been even more fulfilling and meaningful than I could have ever imagined. I firmly believe in the notion of paying it forward, and my hope is that as you read this book, you are better for having done so and that there is at least one takeaway for you that is insightful and transformative.

I wish you all the best on your professional and personal path, and in experiencing your own paradigm shift.

Christina L. Martini

•————————————•

I grew up in Decatur, Illinois, surrounded by lawyers - my father, my oldest sister, two great uncles, many other relatives, all lawyers. Dinner time discussions in my family often centered around my father giving us factual scenarios based on his cases (no names, despite my always asking). Ultimately, those discussions were lessons in critical thinking and analysis, ethics and morals. I looked forward to those discussions, and they were the seeds, planted at an early age, of my desire to follow in my father's footsteps and pursue a career as a plaintiff's personal injury lawyer.

Fast forward a number of years, I graduated from law school and started my career as a personal injury lawyer, first on the defense side, then switching to the plaintiff side six years later. I finally achieved my life's goal. But a funny thing happened on the way to achieving my dream - a couple of years into being a plaintiff's PI attorney, I realized I actually did not enjoy it. I was burned out and knew I could not do that forever. The problem was that I had no Plan B.

After a lot of soul-searching and networking, I decided to try becoming an in-house lawyer. I landed my first in-house job and, with a huge leap of faith, I embarked on an amazing journey that continues to this day. As of this writing, with over 26 years as an in-house generalist, I am still learning, still growing as a lawyer and as a person, and I still love what I do. With that 180° shift in focus re-engineering my career, from personal injury litigation to in-house business generalist, I not only found a way to practice law that I enjoy, I found a way to fulfill my larger purpose: to help improve the lives of my clients and of those I work with in ways that feel genuinely aligned with who I am and what I always wanted to accomplish as a lawyer and in this world.

One of the primary lessons I learned along this journey is that I developed a comfort zone in being outside of my comfort zone. We learn the most from those situations where we face adversity, challenging the ideas and narratives we assume to be true. In such situations and experiences, we are able to test what we are made of and experience monumental paradigm shifts in our lives, relationships and careers.

David G. Susler

LEADERSHIP

Leadership is not about being the loudest person in the room, barking orders or expecting blind obedience from every member of your team. That is not leadership. That is dictatorship. Dictatorship lacks strategic thinking and foresight and is ineffective in the long run. Leadership, on the other hand, is intentional and courageous and, when done right, changes businesses and lives.

The truth is, anyone can play the role of a dictator, clutching power, hoarding credit and using fear as a means of control. But real leadership? That takes courage, consistency and a deep sense of responsibility for the people you serve.

A strong leader does not dominate; they elevate. They do not micromanage; they trust. They do not operate from ego; they act from vision, purpose and a genuine desire to help others succeed.

You can feel the difference when you are around a true leader. People want to follow them, not because they have to, but because they believe in the leader's vision. They feel seen, supported, valued and challenged in the best ways.

Dictators command. Leaders inspire.

Leadership Is not About You—But It Starts with You

To lead well, you must first be committed to growth - your own and everyone else's. That means taking responsibility for your blind spots. It also means learning from failure and continuously investing in building your leadership skills, because no matter how long you have been at it, there is always room for improvement. Being a great leader is not about perfection. It is about presence, purpose and a willingness to grow.

You become a better leader by putting in the work. That can be by reading books written by other great leaders, taking workshops and actively engaging in real-world situations that test your patience, communication skills and resilience. The best leaders have battle scars. They have made mistakes, gotten things wrong and learned what not to do just as often as they have learned what to do.

In one of Christina's earliest leadership roles, she quickly realized that while she appreciated the valuable advice passed down from her predecessors, the only sure way to understand the responsibility of leading others was by figuring things out for herself. *"I had to find my own voice, learn how to navigate conflict, and discover how to lead without trying to control every outcome in ways that felt authentic for me."* That is another thing about great leaders: they understand that there is no one-size-fits-all solution for every situation, and at the end of the day, there is no substitute for showing up and doing the hard work yourself.

Real Leaders Do Not Just Lead Work—They Lead People

Being an expert in your craft matters. A great leader knows what success looks like in their industry and how to navigate the internal dynamics of their organization. But just as critical as technical know-how is the ability to understand people. (There is that EQ again!)

Leadership is about creating and navigating relationships. It requires empathy, the ability to listen deeply, and having the selflessness to put others' needs ahead of your own. It is not about being the most intelligent person in the room. It is about helping others be their best and smartest selves. It is about building a team of people who feel confident, capable and empowered because of your influence, not in spite of it.

Dictators hoard the spotlight. Leaders share it. They give credit generously and surround themselves with other strong, capable people, many of whom could one day succeed them. They are not threatened by that, and in fact, they welcome it.

Strong leaders strive to raise others up, while dictators try to push others down.

Resistance is Not Rebellion

One of the most important things you must accept as a leader is that not everyone will like you.

You can lead with honesty, vision and heart, but still encounter resistance. That does not mean you are failing as a leader. It simply means you are doing something that matters.

Often, the most substantial resistance comes from those most afraid of change. They may have been burned by bad leadership in the past, have their own agenda, feel threatened or simply be stuck in their ways. Your job is not to win them over with charm or to force them into submission; it is to understand where they are coming from, communicate clearly and keep leading despite their resistance or hesitation.

It is usually not personal. It is fear, insecurity or misunderstanding. And sometimes, the most powerful thing you can do as a leader is to meet that resistance with curiosity and compassion rather than defensiveness.

When people feel heard, they soften. And when they feel valued, they show up.

If You Want to Lead, Do Not Wait for Permission

You do not need a title to be a leader. Leadership can start anywhere: on a project team, in a volunteer role, on a committee, or in your community. The key is to take initiative and act with integrity.

Some of the most powerful leadership lessons come from these small moments, when you take the lead on a task, guide a discussion, support a colleague or rally people around a shared goal. These are the places where you build your confidence, practice your voice and shape your own unique leadership style.

If you are in a place that does not offer growth opportunities, do not wait for a promotion that may never come. Instead, create your own path. This might mean deciding to move to a different department or even a new organization. It is imperative that you do not give up on your goals just because someone else is not able to see your full potential.

Great leaders are not handed power. They earn and seize it through consistent action, service and growth.

Strong Leaders Build Strong Cultures

You can often tell when a team has a strong leader. There is a sense of energy, clarity and momentum. People enjoy their work, and they collaborate, communicate and celebrate each other's wins. They all row in the same direction because they believe in the shared vision and their leader.

You can also tell when a team is under weak leadership. Morale is low, people keep their heads down, turnover is high and creativity is absent. The strongest talent often leaves first because great employees will not stick around under poor leadership for long.

Weak leaders stifle innovation, dismiss input, take credit, place blame and avoid accountability. Dictatorship creates disengagement and burnout because no one thrives in an environment where they feel micromanaged, overlooked or undervalued.

On the other hand, strong leaders empower. They listen. They guide. They create a culture where people want to show up and do their best. Not because they are afraid, but because they are inspired.

Leadership Is a Long Game

You do not become a great leader overnight, and you do not stop growing once you get there. Leadership is a continuous process of learning, growing and adapting. It takes vision, resilience and the humility to ask for help, to admit when you are wrong and to continue striving, not for personal glory but for collective success.

Strong leadership is about being nimble and versatile, not rigid or reactive. It is about seeing around the corner - the long game, where the organization is headed, what employees need in order to thrive, and how to best shape a future that is bigger than one person's ambition.

You cannot fake good leadership. People know when it is real, and they feel it in how they are treated, how they are heard and how they are led through both triumphs and challenges.

If you are ready to step into your leadership potential, remember this: You do not need to have all the answers. You simply need to care deeply, act with integrity, and keep showing up. Leadership is not about telling people what to do. It is about showing them what is possible.

Success is Never a One-Person Show

In the early days of our careers, we often think of excellence as a solo act. We pour everything we have into developing our skills, growing our professional knowledge base, and delivering the highest-quality work possible. While those things do matter, they are never the whole picture. It is not until we experience the undeniable momentum that comes from being part of a high-performing team that we realize how much we lack by trying to go it alone. As it turns out, success is never a one-person show - it is a collaborative performance where every player counts.

Collaboration > Individual Achievement

We accomplish exponentially more when we work in tandem with others, not just around them. Many clients and customers might initially be drawn to a specific individual or professional, but their staying power - the reason they return and refer us to others - is often inextricably linked to the team that we create around us. In a high-stakes environment, assembling the right group of people can make or break the outcome.

But great teams do not come together by accident.

High-performing teams are built intentionally, with foresight, self-awareness and emotional intelligence. When they come together, they are more than a group of talented individuals; they are a well-balanced ecosystem where the right mix of skills, communication styles and personalities is aligned to support a shared purpose.

Knowing the People Behind the Performance

Being a strong team player and leader starts with awareness of others and yourself. It requires more than simply knowing someone's job title; it demands an understanding of each team member's unique strengths, areas for improvement, and how they perform both individually and within a group dynamic. A few questions you can ask yourself when creating a high-performing team are:

- Who handles high-pressure moments with grace and ease?

- Who brings creative out-of-the-box solutions when everyone else hits a brick wall?

- Who acts as a quiet anchor to help keep the team and projects grounded?

Effective team leaders (and team members) know when it is time to tag someone in, for what purpose, and how to structure their involvement. Sometimes that means staggering the participation of team members and being mindful of maintaining a balance of personality and energy. Too much of any particular trait is generally not a good thing.

Setting clear roles and expectations is also essential to the performance of a team. When people do not know what is expected of them, it creates friction, insecurity and inefficiency. Transparency is not optional - it is foundational.

The Human Side of Teamwork

No matter how sophisticated the work or how specialized the skills, every high-performing team boils down to one essential component: its people.

People need connection. That means actually talking to one another, not just exchanging emails or direct messages online. As much as we do not want to at times, it is important that we pick up the phone or schedule a face-to-face meeting and check in with our teammates with a moment or two of casual conversation. These human moments build trust and camaraderie among a team. They signal *"We are in this together,"* and that sense of shared ownership is one of the strongest drivers of consistent high performance.

When teammates trust each other, they speak up. They feel comfortable sharing new ideas, voicing concerns and, at times, even disagreeing with the current status quo. As the leader of a high-performing team, it is important to remember that healthy disagreements are a part of the process. Civil, respectful debates about how to best approach a challenge can often lead to better, more creative solutions than any one person could have reached alone. This is where learning happens, bonds are formed and performance excels.

Dynamic, Not Static

High-performing teams are never static. They evolve in real time as people, businesses and client needs evolve. The team that was right last year will likely need to make changes this year, and that is not a sign of failure. It is a sign of responsiveness and evolution.

The most successful teams are built not only around tasks but also around alignment with clients, customers and shared outcomes. It is not about checking boxes; it is about creating synergy. The right mix of skills, styles and mindsets allows high-performing teams to respond quickly and effectively across diverse challenges and opportunities.

Diversity in thought, experience and approach is not just a buzzword. It is a competitive advantage.

Egos Down, Standards Up

High-performing teams are defined by their commitment to a collective standard of excellence. Their focus is not on individual accolades, but on shared successes. That means checking egos at the door and staying aligned with the ultimate goal.

Communication is constant, collaboration is expected and everyone is held accountable, not only for *what* they contribute, but for *how* they contribute. The best teams do not tolerate toxicity or neglect. They hold one another to high standards because they care about each other and the mission. And when it all clicks, it can be transformative.

Leadership Within the Team

Whether you are the official leader or not, your ability to be a valuable teammate matters greatly. A strong team lifts everyone, giving each member the space to grow, lead and evolve. Within a team, it is important to remember that leadership does not mean dominance. It means discernment, knowing when to speak up, when to step back, when to guide, and when to follow.

Strong emotional intelligence is the unspoken currency of high-performing teams. It helps you read the room, anticipate needs and navigate dynamics gracefully. It also helps to build credibility with new team members and maintain harmony during transitions. If you want to lead well, you must start by teaming well.

It's Not Just About Work

Here is the real kicker: when you learn how to be a strong teammate in your professional life, it spills into every other area, including your relationships, your family and your community. You become a better listener, communicate more clearly and offer support without feeling the need to take the spotlight or center stage. Being part of a high-performing team also changes how you move through the world. It teaches you that shared goals build stronger results and more meaningful connections. That trust is built over time and reinforced through small, consistent actions. People matter and ultimately, the best work - the kind that matters - never happens in a vacuum.

RECRUITING AND RETENTION: A SHARED RESPONSIBILITY

Recruiting and retaining talent is one of an organization's most complex and critical challenges. It requires a thoughtful, strategic approach that acknowledges talent management's nuanced, evolving nature. Whether you are on the hiring or candidate side, there is a shared responsibility for making the process productive, meaningful and sustainable.

The Foundations of Talent Management

Talent management is much more than filling seats or posting job openings. It begins with a thorough and honest understanding of your needs and goals, while also being self-aware and honest about your business' strengths and weaknesses. Once you have identified what success looks like for a particular role and for the organization as a whole, you must find and develop people who align with that vision.

Developing talent extends well beyond formal industry training. While substantive, technical skills are essential, soft skills are equally important and are often inextricably linked to emotional intelligence and client service orientation. These "intangibles" frequently determine whether someone will thrive in the culture, and whether they will merely meet or exceed client expectations.

Effective talent management also means ensuring that individuals complement one another, so the strengths of some offset the weaknesses of others. Leadership development and succession planning are crucial to this process, with the need to look at business objectives holistically and assess whether your workforce's skillsets meaningfully align with those objectives.

From Hiring to Development: A Continuum

Hiring the right people is only the first step in the process. Once onboard, ongoing development and training are critical to their success and retention. This means setting clear goals, providing honest, constructive feedback, and proactive career planning. Talent management also requires real-time cooperation and alignment between business strategy and human resources.

This approach helps ensure that you have the right people not only for today's needs but also for the long term. The business world is not static; people grow and change over time. You need to anticipate and support that growth, guiding employees along trajectories that benefit both their careers and the organization's evolving demands. People develop in different ways, and it is important to discern how best to harness each individual's potential, using what you know works well and adapting where it doesn't. Without strong talent management, organizations risk stagnation, talent drain and missed opportunities for growth. Failing to provide the necessary resources, training and growth opportunities, or not giving employees a stake in the organization's success, can often lead to unnecessary turnover. Talent management applies to all employees, not just top performers. Every organization needs leaders and support staff. Neglecting any group can lead to significant organizational decline.

The Cost of Turnover and the Value of Care

Losing valuable employees is not just disruptive - it is also costly in terms of knowledge drain, time and financial impact. It costs far more to replace an employee than to properly train and develop existing ones. If you take care of your employees, they will take care of you and your business.

This mindset fosters loyalty, motivation and a culture where people are empowered to do their best work.

No hiring process can fully guarantee long-term success. Some people shine early on, but are not able to sustain it. Others may not seem like the perfect fit initially, but grow into rock stars with the right amount of support. Not every employee will be right for every organization forever, and that is okay. Meaningful contributions can happen no matter what the tenure, and some employees ultimately find greater success elsewhere. Against this backdrop, it is important to maintain realistic expectations and embrace talent mobility as part of the organizational life cycle.

The Importance of Delegation and Talent Leveraging

Leaders must be willing to meaningfully delegate. The people we hire need opportunities to take on responsibilities, both routine and challenging, to fully develop their skills. It is also essential in building well–leveraged teams to handle the work. Indeed, clients expect having the lowest-cost providers doing the work, and this frees up more senior team members to work on important, high–value tasks that only they can do. Staying attuned to how best to spot and develop talent within our organization and industry is essential. This means analyzing who is succeeding and why, then institutionalizing the practices contributing to that success. Developing talent takes time and commitment, but if done correctly, it can become a competitive advantage.

Hiring Right: Beyond Resumes and Charm

When hiring, it is essential that you clearly identify your team's needs and hire candidates with the right qualifications. Being bright or personable alone does not guarantee a good fit.

Our collective experience has taught us that effective recruiting hinges on asking the right questions. If you feel lukewarm about a candidate, it usually means you should not extend an offer. Evaluating candidates based on how they handle interviews under pressure is just as important as what is on their resumes. Trust your intuition: if something doesn't add up, explore it further, and if the answer remains unsatisfactory, the candidate is not likely a good fit.

Interviewing from Both Sides

Candidates must prepare thoroughly for interviews. Research the organization thoroughly: review public information, speak with current employees, and research with whom you are interviewing. This preparation helps confirm whether the organization and role align with your short- and long-term goals, and demonstrates your genuine interest in the position, setting you apart from other candidates. If you realize during the interview process that a role is not a good fit, be honest with yourself and the potential employer. A positive, realistic approach serves everyone's best interests.

Be yourself. Do not try to guess what the interviewer wants to hear; they will see through it. Ask thoughtful questions. Sometimes, the quality of your questions is the tipping point between equally qualified candidates. Chase what truly interests you, not just what seems like the easiest or most prestigious option.

For the employers out there, it is imperative that you have the right people conduct interviews. They are the face of your organization and must exercise discernment and good judgment. They also need to be friendly, respectful and diplomatic. A consensus on what constitutes a successful hire can help avoid "freestyle interviewing," where decisions are made based on likeability rather than fit. Looking back at past hires can provide valuable insights for moving forward. Identifying common traits in successful employees can help create a predictive index to guide future recruiting efforts.

Beyond Traditional Metrics: Innovating Talent Identification

Michael Lewis' groundbreaking bestseller, *Moneyball,* chronicled the scouting method developed by the Oakland A's General Manager, Billy Beane, that revolutionized how baseball scouts evaluate talent, and its lessons apply to recruiting professionals as well. As in baseball, talent in business is not always apparent at first glance. Just as a player might be more valuable as a pinch hitter than a starter, a professional's actual value emerges in context, through how they align with clients, strategies and team dynamics.

We need to regularly revisit how we define talent and success. Traditional metrics may no longer suffice. As the business world continues to rapidly evolve, we must question whether our long-held assumptions about qualifications, experience and productivity remain valid. In our experience, success depends less on initial promise and more on sustained performance, and on how well we harness strengths and support development over time. We must find individuals capable, committed and open to mentoring, growth and change.

Aligning Talent and Business Needs Over Time

As markets and organizational lifecycles evolve, so do our workforce needs. We must forecast these changes realistically and set clear expectations for how long members of our workforce have to demonstrate value, and to define what success needs to look like.

Just like baseball players get traded or leave as free agents, professionals will often move on to organizations better suited to their skills during particular stages of their careers. Employee mobility is a natural and fundamental part of a healthy recruiting cycle. Recruiting is both an investment in our future, as well as the legacy we leave behind.

Internships: Advice For Success

Internships remain a vital recruitment tool for many organizations. Whether you are applying for or managing internship programs, we have several key insights that can help maximize success:

1. **View the internship as one long interview.** One of the biggest mistakes that summer interns make is believing they have locked in a permanent offer once they land their summer internship. However, many organizations hire more summer interns than they will ultimately need as full-time employees, so their summer program is actually a competition for spots. Moreover, even if you are at a business where there is space for everyone who is hired into the summer program, if you fall short of expectations, you may not get an offer. Therefore, it is imperative that you conduct yourself professionally and do your best at all times.

2. **Take the work seriously.** Summer internships are designed to give students a sense of what it is like to be a full-time member of an organization. It is a mix of work and social activities. Depending on the business, it can seem like a full-time job just to keep up with all the fun. Remember that you need to do a great job on all of your assignments and make sure that you are completing a sufficient number of assignments of the type needed to fully demonstrate and evaluate your capabilities.

3. **Get to know your fellow interns.** Many of us are in relationship-driven businesses. You should make sure you develop strong ties with your fellow summer interns. If all goes well and you receive an offer, you will be working

alongside them after graduation. They can be a great source of often-needed peer guidance and support, particularly during the more challenging times in your career.

4. **Get to know the organization's permanent employees and staff.** The bedrock of every organization is its people. Just as it is important for you to get to know your fellow summer interns, it is equally imperative to develop relationships with the organization's permanent employees and staff. They will be invaluable in helping you learn how to succeed and get things done. You need to have allies who are invested in your success.

5. **Observe the Golden Rule.** It sounds so simple, but it can prove challenging. Demonstrating respect for others is the cornerstone to showing that you have the requisite emotional intelligence to fit within the fabric of the organization. You must do more than just prove that you can do the work - you need to show that you are collaborative, collegial and able to get along with others.

6. **Learn to juggle.** Multitasking is a part of everyday life, especially as a professional. Summer programs are designed to force participants to develop and hone their time management skills and to demonstrate that they can effectively juggle all of the different responsibilities that come with being a successful employee. Be careful about saying "no" to any of the various work and social activities presented to you during the summer.

7. **Find your people.** Being a summer intern can sometimes feel overwhelming, especially as you are starting out and trying to get to know everyone. Be sure to set aside time

every day to walk the halls, and find individuals with whom you meaningfully connect and focus on developing those relationships. It is often by meeting people organically that the best mentoring happens.

8. **Actively seek out feedback.** The best internship programs are designed to provide frequent, comprehensive and honest feedback. Beyond whatever formal tools there may be, take the opportunity to speak directly with those giving you assignments and those who are running the program to hear their comments firsthand and take their suggestions to heart. The information they provide will be helpful, and you will be seen as engaged and proactive about your career.

9. **Learn from your mistakes.** We all make mistakes, and no one is perfect. What is important is that we learn from them. When something does not go as planned, you should take a step back, figure out what happened and how to do it better the next time, and then be sure to adjust your approach accordingly.

10. **Is this the right place for me?** Many organizations have a rigorous interview process before deciding who to hire into their summer programs. The hope is that by the end of the summer, the intern's performance has in large part validated these choices. That being said, it sometimes becomes clear over the course of the summer that certain people may not be a good long-term fit. These decisions should be a two-way street, meaning that both the organization and the summer intern need to exercise sound judgment during the course of the summer in determining whether the relationship is going to work. It is better to

make that evaluation before certain career-changing decisions are made.

Recruiting and retention are ongoing, dynamic institutional processes that demand intentionality, openness and care. By approaching them as shared responsibilities, with clear strategies and honest communication, we can build a workplace where people can thrive, contribute and succeed in the long run, no matter the outcome.

Client Service: The Key to Success

Client service is receiving more attention and is incredibly important, particularly as the delivery of legal services continues to evolve. As a result, attorneys in private practice are competing much more aggressively for clients, and there is increased awareness that one of the most important things that distinguishes attorneys from one another is the level and quality of attention they give to their clients. Client service is the meaningful differentiator between good lawyers and great lawyers. It is the biggest thing clients remember about their experiences with a particular lawyer.

Client service is so much more than having a deep knowledge of the substantive area in which you practice and being able to get to the right legal answer. It focuses on taking that legal advice, viewing it holistically and putting it into a context that enables the client to make a sound business decision for their organization. While providing quality work remains of upmost importance, client service places a particular emphasis on developing more of a partnership and a collaborative relationship with your client. Just as it is important for outside counsel to provide outstanding client service to their clients, it is equally important for in-house attorneys to do the same with their business colleagues.

Emotional intelligence skills are a critical part of successful client service, including empathy, effective communication and listening skills, optimism and a proficiency at inspiring confidence and trust. The moment a client seeks advice regarding a new matter and the staffing process begins, it is prudent to include team members who have experience with, and institutional knowledge of, the client, since they can offer invaluable insight and guidance. They can also help frame the relevant issues in a way that draws upon past experiences with the client, their working style, their likes and dislikes, their strengths and challenges and their victories and defeats. Indeed, this is a unique value add that other team members may simply not be in a position to provide and which makes a world of difference when measuring the team's overall performance and effectiveness. To the extent that the matter is a new client engagement, it is important to determine who on the team has relevant substantive and business sector experience.

From the moment that a new engagement begins, attorneys should be evaluating not only what the client relevant legal issues are, but also the frame of reference of their primary client contact, both with respect to the matter at hand as well as within the context of the corporation or business unit in which they work. It is also important to determine who else within the client's business may be affected by the issue and whether it is necessary to involve them in any decision-making process. Budget and timing considerations should also be openly discussed and a preliminary plan developed so that there is consensus from the beginning and a framework within which to have continuing conversations regarding these parameters, particularly in the event the approach needs to be tweaked.

As the matter intake process progresses, lawyers need to determine not only how they are going to substantively address the legal issues at hand, but also how to package the results in a way that is most meaningful and helpful to the client. This requires a delicate balance between technical skills and emotional intelligence. Attorneys should confirm that they have the required expertise and knowledge to properly address both the legal and business perspectives, and determine whether they need to line up additional resources on the client service team, particularly as a matter evolves. Lawyers must be self-aware enough to recognize when bringing others into a matter may better serve the client than trying to do the work oneself, even if the project is within one's general practice area. Ultimately, doing what is best for the client, both in terms of quality and value, preserves and strengthens a client relationship, and includes not doing work yourself that is better done by someone else. Do not let your fear or insecurity about introducing other people to your client drive you to make decisions that are not in the client's best interest.

Once the client team is formed, the team leader must properly communicate the project scope, clearly define each member's role, conduct the necessary risk assessments, and effectively manage the project from all relevant angles. At this juncture, it is critically important to assess the exact nature of the necessary deliverables, beyond just the legal advice itself. Indeed, sometimes a client is seeking moral support or personal advice in tandem with the legal advice, and the high EQ lawyer will sense this and effectively serve as the trusted advisor that the client needs.

As the project winds down and the team prepares to advise the client, it is always prudent to take a step back and assess the team's performance and to consider the best way to deliver the advice. Every client and situation is unique, thereby requiring a carefully tailored approach. Ultimately, one must consider the impact the advice will have on various constituents within the organization, whether additional decision-makers and stakeholders need to be informed and whether the conclusion will require further research and evaluation. Even if the project has reached its natural end, high EQ dictates that attorneys follow up and seek feedback to ensure the client is satisfied.

The business world continues to rapidly evolve and this is the environment in which clients are forced to operate. The end result is a buyer's market for legal services where clients are requesting more for less and greater value than ever before. They are demanding more business-focused creativity from their lawyers. They are also demanding approaches to problem-solving which are more as a strategic business partner and advisor than an arms-length service provider. Clients also want their attorneys to significantly invest in their relationship. This means a strong commitment to developing the qualities and characteristics that drive all healthy relationships, including trust, loyalty and communication.

These client needs have brought about a more sophisticated relationship between in-house and outside counsel. David explains, *"I think the majority of in-house lawyers are interested in truly collaborative partnerships with their outside counsel. Successful outside counsel understand that, ultimately, we should be aligned with the same goals."*

Building Strong Client Relationships

Clients want sophisticated legal advice that is customized to their specific business needs and takes into account their risk tolerance. They also want their lawyers to deliver great value to their businesses, and they expect strong service. Lawyers need to understand that these concepts - great legal advice, value and exceptional service - mean different things to different people, so the trick is to figure out how each client defines them and how to strike the right balance so that the relationship is a success. The right blend of these characteristics constantly shifts within a given relationship. It is important for lawyers to be sensitized to these dynamics and to adjust their approach accordingly.

Whether the lawyer is retained for a single, discrete matter or an ongoing engagement, clients want targeted advice, delivered quickly, conscientiously, for as low cost as possible. Clients want their lawyers to help them solve their problems and help them manage risk to maximize business potential. They want their lawyers to be available when needed and to make them feel like they are their most important client. They want trusted advisors and to know their lawyers always have their backs.

There are a number of things which can jeopardize a relationship. Ultimately, they are all symptoms of a lawyer not meeting their client's needs and expectations. Over-promising and under-delivering is one of the most common mistakes. Giving legal advice in a vacuum and failing to adapt to the changing legal and business landscapes are additional missteps. Poor communication can also be a key mistake because of the potential consequences, including an inability to really hear and understand what a client is saying. These are the cornerstones of creating and maintaining a successful client relationship.

Another huge mistake is lying to a client. Don't do it. Poor billing hygiene, such as billing too much for tasks, or for things you should never bill for in the first place, is another quick way to lose your client's trust. For example, if a company's general counsel asks outside counsel to prepare a proposal for handling certain matters going forward, do not bill for that time spent. Another huge mistake is neglecting your client. Do not let your client think you have forgotten about them or their matter by going radio silent for long stretches of time. Check in once in a while, even if just to say, *"Nothing is happening, but here is what and when to expect something."*

Changing Conversations

The dialogue between in-house and outside lawyers has shifted considerably over the years, much in the same way that the practice of law has evolved. Bottom line: there are a lot more expectations in communication around the relationship, and what outside counsel is expected to deliver to in-house attorneys. There is a lot less tolerance for ambiguity, particularly around cost. For example, if there is a cost overrun for a particular project, outside counsel are expected to shoulder that risk much more frequently now than they used to.

Clients also really want to know up front who is going to be working on the project, beyond the relationship partner. They want to know how much time is going to be spent by the different levels of attorneys and other professionals, both as a cost check and to develop a rapport with the whole team.

The client's expectations around the final work product are also key. Sometimes the client is expecting a luxury car, sometimes they are expecting a scooter, and sometimes they are expecting a skateboard. It depends on the circumstances the client is in, what they need and can afford.

There are several important factors in getting to the root of your client's needs. First, you need to understand the issues your client is facing and the legal and business implications of those issues. To get to the heart of those issues, you must have open and honest communication with your client. You have to be able to ask the necessary questions and be willing and able to listen to the client's answers and hear what they are saying.

The correct legal answer only gets you halfway, since there is always a business context within which issues are addressed and decisions are made. There are also other factors, such as the client's organizational politics, which play an important role. Lawyers need to be sensitive to these dynamics and be able to strike the correct balance so that the advice they provide is from the most practical and constructive point of view for the client.

From Christina's perspective:

"One of my favorite aspects of this whole topic is the human interaction, right brain, intuitive angles to these conversations. The clients really need to feel like they are being heard. And they have to feel like their outside counsel is actively engaged in the conversation. If clients do not feel like their outside counsel really want to help them at the end of the day, and are just running the clock and wanting to get paid, I think that really shifts the conversation in a way that ends up hurting the client relationship. Sometimes what is not said is more important than what is said. Clients are charged with figuring out which of their outside counsel is driving value to the business and who is really driving great results. And there is an expectation among clients that their attorneys are going to be willing to take the time to understand their business. That they are going to be willing to make an investment, both in terms of time and emotion."

From David's perspective:

"The changes I have seen in the conversation really relate more to the structural elements of the relationship: more discussion about budgets, more discussion about alternative fees, more discussion about value, and evaluating the relationship. And I think these changes in the conversation are positive. They bring about value in the profession, generally, and in the attorney-client relationship in particular. If the conversations are had in the spirit of openness, honesty and trust, then it really is a win-win situation."

If you are having a fully transparent conversation and you are talking about different aspects of the relationship, you can gain greater budgetary certainty, better planning, and better overall communication, leading to a stronger overall relationship. These discussions can be difficult to initiate, especially if you have never had them before. But they are actually much easier to have than people might think. Resources such as the Association of Corporate Counsel (ACC) Value Challenge provide a terrific model in which to hold these dialogues. It outlines the beginning of the conversation, and it helps to frame the conversation in a mutually valuable way. It should be noted, these conversations are not just about cutting outside counsel fees. They are about shifting and restoring value to that relationship. It is about the processes and mechanisms that you can engage in to build value, which in turn lead to a stronger, healthier, longer-term relationship.

If you have not been actively having these discussions, or if you have not changed the conversations you have been having with your outside counsel or your in-house client, then we urge you to start. David explains, *"Two things I look for in hiring and staying with outside counsel are creativity and proactivity. If you initiate that conversation, you are demonstrating both of those things to me."* The worst thing that can happen is your client says, *"No thanks, I am really happy with the way things are."* But if you kick it off with simple questions like: *"Have you ever considered alternative fee arrangements?"* or *"How are we doing?"* that can lead to a more open and deeper discussion about things you have probably never discussed before, or at least not anything you have discussed in depth. And that can only bring about a positive change in the relationship.

Improving Your Communication Skills to Become a Better Lawyer

Communication skills are at the heart of every great lawyer, and they are a lawyer's currency. As with most things, the more you practice, the better you become at it. It takes a lot of hard work to be a good communicator, and it helps to have strong mentors to help you hone your skills. Much of oral and written legal communications is taking a lot of information and distilling it down into a clear and concise message that clients can understand, while steering them in a particular direction. Regardless of how you are communicating with your clients, it is important to carefully think about what you are going to say before you say it. You should consider not only whether the message is substantively correct but also whether you are saying it as effectively as possible.

You also need to think about your client's preferred style and method of communication. Everyone has different styles which need to be respected. When you are meeting with your client, outline what you are going to say in advance to help get you started. When you are writing to them, carefully think about and proofread what you have written.

One of the best ways to improve your communication skills is to listen - listen to other lawyers, and listen to your clients, not only to what they say but also to how they say it. There is a physical aspect to oral communication, which is as important as what you say, if not more so. Observe other's body language, how they deliver their words, in court, in client meetings and on the phone. Observe their facial expressions and gestures. Listen to their tone of voice and modulation.

The more you speak, the better of a communicator you will become, so practice that as well - speak at conferences, client meetings and board meetings. The bottom line is practice. And remember - you can always improve, no matter how long you have been practicing.

As with any relationship, there are both good communication practices between clients and outside counsel, and poor. It is an attorney's responsibility to gauge the proper cadence and scope of the communications that their clients expect. Every client is different, as is every matter. Outside counsel should ask the right questions and also have an intuitive sense as to what is appropriate in a given situation. This will help eliminate issues around poor communication such as communicating too much or not enough; making significant decisions without discussing them with the client first; and failing to properly prioritize developments in the matter for the client's consideration. There is often an optimal rhythm of communication, and it is outside counsel's responsibility to figure that out.

Another bad habit is not being communicative with your client at all and allowing the monthly invoice to double as a status report. There is little worse than a client receiving a bill for work they had no idea was being done, especially when it involves important developments and decisions.

There is a delicate balance between tracking the status of a project and micromanaging the work, particularly since one client's idea of micromanaging is another's belief that you are doing a great job. Our advice is to stay close to your clients and get a good sense of what they want and need.

Micromanagement happens when you do not fully trust or have confidence in the people with whom you are working. We recommend that you work with professionals whom you respect and trust so that this does not happen.

From David's perspective:

"I tend to be actively involved in all matters assigned to outside counsel but try not to micromanage. The level of my involvement in a particular engagement often is a matter of importance and trust. If I feel like I have to micromanage my outside counsel, push them to move them along or ask for an update, it likely means there is a trust issue and trouble brewing. If the lines of communication are open and flowing, this is not an issue."

Dealing With Opposing Counsel

It is essential that you are calm, cool, collected and respectful in your communications with an adversary, no matter how contentious the situation may be. You should try to avoid taking an inflammatory tone in your communications, since it is generally unnecessary and can often make the situation more difficult. People will mistake the need to deliver a strong message with yelling or screaming to get it across. Strong messages are generally best delivered in a calm, direct manner. As in your dealings with clients, it is also important to try to see the other side's point of view as best as you can. By putting yourself in their shoes, you will have a greater understanding of where they are coming from. By doing your best to fully appreciate both sides of an issue, you will be better positioned to reach a satisfactory resolution to the matter at hand.

Implicit in effectively communicating to the other side is first understanding what your client's goals are. You will encounter a number of different styles in opposing counsel, some easier to deal with than others, and you have to learn to roll with whatever you get. We strongly believe in the old adage that you attract more flies with honey than with vinegar.

Defining Value in Legal Services

Since time immemorial, product and service providers have been evaluated based on various criteria, both quantitative and qualitative. While certain offerings such as the proverbial widget more readily lend themselves to quantitative evaluations, value-based discussions have increasingly focused on professional services such as accounting, consulting and the law. We can all learn from those industries which have historically made purchasing decisions based on optimization analyses and processes.

From Christina's perspective:

"As both an industrial engineer and a lawyer, I have a deep understanding of the desire to standardize procurement evaluations for legal services through a more disciplined, consistent framework. But just as there are advantages to applying these methodologies in this context, there are also inherent limitations, particularly when they are used in lieu of a more qualitative analysis of the more nuanced facets of a particular legal provider's offerings."

At the cornerstone of these evaluations lies the concept of value. Value is defined as the relationship between the perceived benefits of an offering as compared to its cost. This relationship can be expressed as a benefits-to-costs ratio. If that ratio has a value greater than one, the benefits outweigh the costs, and if it is less than one, the costs outweigh the benefits. While this analysis seems easy, it is not as simple as it looks. Indeed, the concept of price is often mistakenly conflated with the idea of value, although they are by no means the same. While price is one factor, there are many other important considerations which are given insufficient weight, or completely overlooked in the process. A few of these are included here:

1. **Relevant experience and efficiency.** These are critical to the legal services value analysis. The more experienced we are, the better we understand the critical facets of a particular issue, and the more we can contribute. We will also bring a more heightened level of efficiency to the engagement than a less experienced lawyer, which is also very important when determining our value proposition.

2. **Understanding the client's business.** There are a variety of ways to achieve this, including having a consistent, experienced team servicing the client across all of its legal needs. If the engagement is new, we should invest the time to get to know the client's business and understand its unique likes, dislikes and pressure points. Having relevant sector experience can be very helpful in winning the business and getting a jump start.

3. **Client service excellence.** This is a must if we are trying to differentiate ourselves from the competition. Important considerations include ensuring there is consistent alignment with our client's work product expectations, as well as being as accessible to our clients as they need us to be.

4. **Sound judgment.** As lawyers, we are regularly asked to express our legal views regarding various issues. Being able to consistently express sound judgment, particularly in moments of crisis and

outside of our specific area of expertise, will make the difference between being a good lawyer and a great one.

5. **Keeping the lines of communication open.** This is essential in ensuring a client's needs are well met. We should carefully gauge the nature and cadence of our client's communication styles and adjust our approach accordingly. Our clients should also provide us with the necessary information and cues to enable us to effectively make these assessments and to adjust our approach as needed.

6. **Correct our approach in real time**. Great lawyers are able to regularly evaluate their performance and determine what they are doing well and what they need to work on. If we find that a certain approach is not particularly effective, we should not wait until our client says something - we should correct it in real time, before the client even sees it.

7. **Seeing around the corner.** Mastering the art of prognostication is priceless. Clients highly value our ability to keep tabs on all the moving pieces of a particular situation and to play out likely outcomes a few steps ahead of the game and to advise them accordingly.

8. **Taking the long-term view of the relationship.** Every client relationship is unique. Sometimes they start off slowly or in a narrow niche, and at times there may be more in it for the client than for us. If we are willing to take a long-term view of the relationship, we will increase our chances of being able to realize the longer-term upside and to better monetize the relationship.

9. **Success is a two-way street.** As in all good relationships, there is a give and take with clients. Generally, their needs come before our own. At the same time, we must run our business responsibly. While

there may not be alignment across all of our service offerings and a particular client's needs, effectively striking that balance will solidify our credibility and help ensure the longevity of the relationship.

10. **Inspiring trust.** While being trustworthy is a critical component of inspiring trust, we must also demonstrate our ability to seamlessly weave together capabilities, project an inner confidence, and have a commanding presence, particularly when meeting prospective clients. This will enable us to demonstrate our ability to serve as a trusted advisor, which is another significant differentiator.

Finding the Right Answer, and Answering the Tough Questions

The right answer is more than simply reciting applicable law, whether one is working with business clients on commercial deals or individuals on their personal matters. Ultimately, the right answer for clients is the answer that best serves the client's needs at the moment. Determining what the client needs depends on the facts and circumstances of the given matter, which includes a broad range of considerations.

The right answer depends on the client, the issue, how important the issue is to the client, and who will ultimately make the business decision. The right answer for one client may be completely wrong for another, and the right answer today may be the wrong answer tomorrow. It can also depend on where the client's organization is in its lifecycle. The right answer is generally the best answer one can get to under the circumstances, and is not just the correct legal answer. It also takes into account the political and business dynamics at play.

The process of working with clients to get to the right answer requires a few key considerations. You need to determine what the right answer is from a legal perspective, assuming there is one. You then need to consider the business and political dynamics that are at play for the client, and you need to know who the ultimate decision-makers and influencers are and how they will go about making the call. You also need to consider whether there is a track record for making these types of decisions and what the best- and worst-case scenarios are. The client's risk tolerance and the timeline within which a client needs to get to an answer are important too.

The best way to start is by trying to ascertain what the client truly needs. This begins with learning the relevant facts and a discussion about the client's goals. Then it is a matter of discerning how those goals mesh with the reality of the facts and law. Sometimes this means having a conversation with the client about possibly modifying their expectations, tempering them or perhaps expanding them, as well as discussing pertinent legal and business realities, often drawing upon your own career experiences. These conversations with clients - discussing and debating facts and law and ultimately reaching the right answer - can be some of the most rewarding aspects of your practice.

You need to know and understand your client. Putting yourself in their shoes can help tremendously - but you also need to take yourself out of the equation at a certain point and not make the right answer for the client be about what the right answer is for you. This is particularly true when it comes to issues such as risk tolerance, where the client may be willing to take bigger risks than we would or vice versa.

Timing is also key. The right answer for a client is generally the best answer you can get to with limited knowledge and often under extenuating circumstances. You often have to feel your way through it and rely on what past experience has taught you in similar situations. You should also remember the importance of asking the right questions. Do not be afraid to ask questions and to seek help and guidance, especially if the issue is outside your area of practice. Finally, remember that there generally is no one right answer, and what we are really talking about is the best answer under existing time constraints which more than anything is an optimization exercise across a number of different variables.

The number one lesson is to listen to your client. This involves more than listing a recitation of the facts. You must hear their concerns, goals, passion for the matter, urgency, commitment and understanding, or lack thereof, about the situation. Discuss and explain potential outcomes, positives and negatives and assess risk. Do not simply say *"no"* - offer alternatives. Temper your black letter legal advice with business and life realities.

Number two, put your ego aside. You may think you know the right answer but so may your client. In the business/commercial context, your client knows his or her business better than you do. However, your client may not readily know or appreciate the right answer in a legal context. As the attorney, we must guide our clients to the right answer by engaging in the right conversations. Remember to revisit these conversations because the right answer may change as a matter progresses, and do not be afraid to change course with your advice.

There are a couple of scenarios in which you may need to tell your client that you do not know the answer to their question. The first is when the client is asking a question outside of your substantive area. The second is when the issue is in your practice area, but the client is asking for a level of certainty that you may not be able to deliver off the cuff. When the client asks you, *"Can I do this?"* or *"Will I get sued if I do that?"* for an issue in your practice area, depending on the circumstances, those can be very tough questions to answer. Christina explains, *"More often than not, even if I do not have 100% certainty, I am able to get the client to a level of certainty that enables them to make the business decision they need to make given the legal risk presented."*

When you are talking about an issue outside of your specialty, you may or may not have a gut reaction about it. Generally, we will tell the client that we need to do some additional legwork to get them the answer they need. Clients are generally very appreciative of this candor, and would much rather you be honest in these situations.

David explains, *"If it is a more technically discrete area, I will tell my client I need to consult with outside counsel and get back to them, and there is no problem with that."* Lawyers cannot really give a 100% absolute answer all the time. Our job ultimately is to manage risk. Our clients are sophisticated businesspeople and they understand that risk is an inherent element of doing business. They are looking to us to give them the confidence to know that a risk is acceptable and appropriately managed. While we sometimes have to tell clients that we do not know what the right answer is, we have also developed trust and credibility, and they know that even if we need to do research or consultation, ultimately, we will give them sound advice.

Above all else, provide the type of client service you would want.

From Christina's perspective:

"When it comes to issues that I am not immediately familiar with, there are a couple of buckets that those fall into. The first are those issues that fall within my practice area that I might not have an immediate answer to. In those cases, what I will typically do is pull a treatise or do some quick online research, or I will talk to a colleague who is in my practice area who may have dealt with that specific issue. If we are talking about issues that are outside my practice area, given that I am at a global firm with many hundreds of attorneys who have different specialty areas, often the quickest and most cost-effective way for me to get answers to those questions is to pick up the phone and talk to somebody with that specialty. Even when I am dealing with issues where ultimately another partner in my firm will handle the matter, I still stay involved, especially if I am the relationship partner for that particular client."

From David's perspective:

"I have a strong foundation to draw upon when I confront new matters I have not handled before. I ask enough questions to make sure I understand the issue. Depending on what the matter is, I might do some online research, or put out some questions on one of my lawyer listservs and seek feedback from other in-house attorneys. I will also draw upon my experience. Even if I have not dealt with the exact matter before, I will likely have dealt with something similar. If it is a complex area requiring a depth

of knowledge I do not have, then I will go to outside counsel who has that expertise.

It is rare that any issue I deal with is purely legal, but usually a mix of legal and business. I will often talk to the businesspeople in my company and make sure I understand the business aspects of the matter. This is where being in-house gives me a distinct advantage because I have direct access to the business folks. Handling issues I've never dealt with before, for me, is where the fun is. The ability to conquer new matters I have never dealt with before is how I grow as an attorney to become a better counselor and advisor."

Clients need their lawyers to understand where they are coming from and what they are trying to accomplish. They should take full ownership of their work and view the relationship as a partnership. This attitude means that outside counsel view their client's problems as their own, so if there is an issue keeping the client awake at night, outside counsel should also be losing sleep. In-house counsel also expect their outside counsel to understand their business and to be able to put themselves in their client's shoes. They want creativity - to think outside the box and to come up with innovative, thoughtful solutions to get the business where it wants to go. Finally, in-house counsel want their attorneys to prioritize what is in the client's best interest.

From David's perspective:

"As an in-house attorney, I am both the client - with outside counsel, and the attorney serving clients - my business colleagues within my company. I work hard to deliver top-notch work product and also to provide a level of service that enables them to do their job more easily and effectively. I also practice with the goal of leaving my clients with a positive impression of lawyers and the profession. I work hard to make sure they understand I am part of their team and part of the solution to help keep our business flourishing. For example, I learn their operational needs and

explain how the legal aspects of the matter facilitate or hinder our business. If I have to say no to something, I do not stop there but also bring solutions that will help close the deal and ensure the business continues moving forward. I strive to make my client look good and succeed in their job and leave them feeling that I made a positive difference."

Helping Clients Assess Risk

There are several important steps in helping a client assess risk. First, since risk needs to be examined within the construct of a particular circumstance, you need to begin by properly defining the situation. You also need to understand the different facets of the issue, what the legal ramifications are and the business considerations at hand. This includes having a deep understanding of what the business ultimately wants to accomplish and how those plans and desires may be at odds with the path of acceptable risk for the company. You must also understand the level of risk the client is willing to take. Ultimately, you need to help the client to balance the trade-offs between accomplishing the business goals and mitigating risk. Christina explains, *"I think of reaching this balance as tuning a radio and dialing it up or down depending on what the client's risk tolerance is."*

Often, certain aspects of a client's circumstances will make it difficult to assess risk. This includes, for example, when the situation is evolving quickly, and it is hard to know exactly where things stand at any given moment. Furthermore, when a lot is at stake with a decision, it can often lead to key stakeholders waffling, which can make it more difficult to reach a decision. Having a lot on the line can also make it hard to determine who the ultimate decision-makers are. Also, if there are a number of significant unknowns in the situation, or if the client's risk tolerance keeps shifting, it can also be difficult to reach a decision.

It can also be a challenge getting the client to understand both the business and legal risks. Another challenge is in not having all of the facts, and simply not having control of all outcomes.

There are a number of things that you can do to help your clients properly analyze and make decisions in the face of risk. First, you and your client should be as fluid as possible with decision-making and understand that you are in a dynamic environment and circumstances may change a lot during the process. You need to make sure that you are working with the right person at your client's organization who has the ultimate authority to make the decision, or who at least has direct access to these people. Seek out the information and people you need to best help your client make a decision that is consistent with its risk tolerance, and be sure that you fully understand what that risk tolerance is. Understand the potential ripple effects of the risk presented and the ultimate decision reached, and the overall impact. Finally, you need to be prepared, expect the unexpected, and allow for some wiggle room.

Happy Clients

Driving client satisfaction is more of an art than a science. The idea is simple - we should all do what is necessary to keep our clients happy. We all know this can be much more difficult than it seems. What makes one client happy can drive another crazy, and while a particular working style may be ideal for some, it may be completely unacceptable to others. As with most things, there is no one-size-fits-all approach to keeping clients happy. It involves carefully weighing myriad factors and striking a delicate balance across various levers. By doing so, we can more effectively nurture and grow our client relationships, so that they endure over the long run.

The following are just a few of the many important considerations in keeping clients happy:

1. **Know your client and understand their business.** We hear this all the time. Nevertheless, when we read client satisfaction surveys and about general counsel pet peeves, these are major issues time and again. Empathy plays an important part in effectively leading client relationships and understanding how clients see our

performance. Clients are people too, and we need to put ourselves in their shoes when evaluating how we are doing. We must keep up with current events in their businesses and in their sectors to understand the business context in which their issues arise.

2. **Deliver great client service.** This is another client pet peeve. Great service goes hand in hand with understanding our clients and their businesses. It is incumbent upon us to gather the clues when discussing projects and discerning the business context in which they arise. The more effective we are at leveraging this information, the better we are at consistently delivering what our clients want and need.

3. **Know your client's pressure points.** We all have them - those things in life that drive us crazy. Whether it is litigation, an important transaction, or a run of the mill project, we must figure out what our client's pressure points are so we know how to effectively navigate the landmines of a particular situation and so that we can serve as better advocates and trusted advisors.

4. **Don't be tone deaf.** Effective communication skills are essential in every client relationship. This means knowing when to talk and - even more important - when to listen. It also means truly hearing what is being said, even when nothing is being said at all. Some clients are very outgoing and communicative, while others are more quiet and reserved. Whatever the case may be, we need to adapt to our client's communication styles and recognize that they can vary widely from one person to the next. This enables us to react appropriately in any given situation.

5. **Don't be a used car salesman.** All clients understand that outside counsel need to sell their services to be successful. Much of this effort is directed to existing clients. Indeed, studies in business

development strategies have shown that there is a much higher likelihood of driving additional work from existing clients than creating new relationships from scratch. Being effective in business development requires a certain amount of gravitas and finesse, as well as knowing when to put the pedal to the metal and when to ease up. Clients expect outside counsel to be realistic and to discern the right time and place to try to generate more business, and the right services to pitch. Under no circumstances should we be selling them the wrong make or model. It will annoy the client and diminish our credibility.

6. **Be confident, not arrogant.** Clients hire outside counsel to accomplish those things that they cannot do on their own. A critical component of a client's hiring decision is whether the attorney under consideration inspires and projects confidence. This is particularly important with high-stakes projects where we are being asked to do the impossible, or where millions of dollars are on the line. At times like these, being meek or insecure will not serve us well. But we also need to know when humility and a softer approach are in order. Being able to dial the confidence meter up or down depending on the circumstances is an integral part of successful relationship management.

7. **Be proactive.** Clients rely on us to clearly and carefully map the ways in which a particular issue may play out and to promptly prepare them for the good, the bad and the ugly. We must draw from our professional experiences and leverage them to be as proactive as possible. We should also tap our intuition for our clients' benefit. If we have misgivings about something, we have to figure out why that is and timely advise our clients.

8. **Know your strengths and weaknesses.** No matter how great we may be at certain things, we simply cannot be good at everything,

and we can always improve various aspects of our performance. Being aware of our strengths and weaknesses enables us to figure out our sweet spots, and where we may need someone else's assistance to navigate through certain situations and circumstances. Ultimately, we will improve our success with clients and our organization's top-line revenue by making sure we have the right horses in the race.

There are other resources that can help with your client relationships. If you know lawyers who have experience working with certain clients, they can provide you with valuable insight that you might not otherwise have. You can also reach out to experienced practitioners and mentors to get some general advice, and also do some research about your clients to better understand their businesses, successes and challenges. Finally, you should take a step back and think about how you would approach being the client and what you would want from your outside counsel. It is always helpful to put yourself in their shoes to predict their approach and needs.

What is unique for in-house counsel is that they are both clients as well as attorneys for the internal business teams. The challenge is to delicately walk the line as both lawyer and employee. You must remember that your legal duty runs to the company, not to any individual employee, which is not always easy.

Socializing for Success

Professional success hinges on a few factors, including the quality of the relationships that you have with your colleagues and clients. It is very difficult to build alliances and to develop the trust and credibility that comes with them unless you put yourself in situations where you are able to meaningfully interact with others and get to know them better. Work functions are often the easiest way to do just that. Having a level of comfort with your colleagues helps ensure that they will think of you the next time they have an issue that is within your area of expertise, and vice versa. It also facilitates other types of workplace collaboration, including leadership, business development, recruiting and integration activities.

These connections are critically important. People need to know you, like you and trust you or they will not want to work with you. Socializing and attending work functions together helps establish rapport and credibility with your clients and colleagues that are critically important to success on every level. When done with an open mind, such activities not only help build business, they can also enhance job satisfaction.

Partnering With the Business

Partnering with the business means working hand in hand with people at the client to effectively work through and manage both the legal and business aspects of a project. Whether our client contact is in the legal department or is a businessperson, it is all about understanding their priorities, objectives, strengths, weaknesses, pressure points and best- and worst-case scenarios. It is also understanding how each of these is defined for the client as an organization may be different from how our point of contact chooses to define them for themselves.

It can also be thought of as becoming an integral part of the business team, a valued partner in operations, development and strategy. David explains, *"I work as closely with our business teams as possible, from the senior most leadership on down, so that I learn as much as possible about every aspect of the business, including how our factories operate, what our customers' products are and our overall industry landscape."* The greater your understanding of these details and the big picture, the better lawyer you are for your company and clients, and a more valued and trusted partner for your colleagues.

Issues may arise if you are not picking up on the cues that your client is giving you, either directly or indirectly, about how they feel the situation would best be handled. Since the correct legal answer may not always align with how the client wants a situation to turn out, you need to be clear on the client's position so that you can adjust your approach accordingly. As part of that, you need to understand that if you find that the answer is "no" when the client has already decided to move forward, you should then quickly shift the conversation to one about risk mitigation, rather than just saying "no." You need to remember that as the lawyer advising the business, it is ultimately not your decision to make.

In sum, exceptional client service is not a luxury - it is every client's expectation, and its presence or absence is evident, no matter who the client is. The following tips will help maximize your effectiveness with clients, thereby deepening your existing relationships and facilitating your development of new ones.

- **Honor your word** - Clients will evaluate you and your services based on what you actually do on their behalf, not on what you intend to do or say you will do. Ultimately, clients will judge you based on how well your actions align with the expectations you have created in their minds, especially when their management is holding them accountable for your performance. There is nothing worse than overpromising and underdelivering.

- **Be responsive** - Clients both appreciate and expect their attorneys to be responsive, even during evenings, weekends, vacations, and while traveling. They also expect timely follow-ups once their immediate needs have been addressed. Business happens 24/7, 365 days a year, and attorneys need to be just as responsive as their clients are required to be. You can be a terrific lawyer, but if you are not there when your clients need you, you may as well be mediocre.

- **Listen to your clients** - Listening is a critical skill, particularly when getting assignments and receiving feedback from clients. You need to be able to hear and process what they are saying, recalibrate your approach to the extent necessary, and go back to your client promptly to communicate solutions. Even in challenging situations, you can strengthen your relationship if you are thoughtful and strategic in how you react and communicate.

- **Go the extra mile** - You must be generous with your time and genuine in your willingness to help your clients, even if you do not reap immediate rewards. Successful business is all about relationships which are cultivated and deepened over time and through connecting with others in a meaningful way.

- **Build a strong team** - You cannot do it all alone; you need to hire and mentor your team to understand, appreciate and develop strong client service. You are only as good as your team, and teams are more effective when everyone cooperates, participates, collaborates and brings others along.

- **Build on your strengths** - It is always important to be open to feedback, both positive and negative, and to learn and grow through professional and life experiences. It is just as important to celebrate your strengths, and to determine effective ways to leverage those talents as much as possible, rather than focusing on remedying your weaknesses. You cannot be everything to everybody and, at a certain point, trying to do so becomes counterproductive.

- **Be empathetic** - Effective client service requires you to always put yourself in your client's shoes and think about how you would feel if you were facing the issue at hand, both from substantive and contextual standpoints. Often, it is not just a legal problem that needs to be addressed; there is also a business context within which the issue arises which requires just as much attention and consideration.

- **Focus on the deliverable and the audience** - Package your work product with care, and remember that reaching the right answer is often only half the battle. Figuring out the framework within which to deliver the advice can make all the difference in whether the client will consider your performance a success. Is your client looking for a bottom line, no-frills answer, or do they need something more formal and elaborate? Who at the client organization is the ultimate audience for your advice? What kind of relationship do they have with your client contact, and where do those individuals fit within the context of both the issue at hand and the organization as a whole?

- **Stay positive and be authentic** - Clients can tell when you are being open, honest, authentic and trustworthy, and they are much more likely to respond in a loyal way. If you are pretending to be someone you are not and do not genuinely care and put your clients first, it is obvious, and clients respond accordingly. Being positive and upbeat is just as important, and showing that you love what you do will make you more attractive to both existing and potential clients.

- **It is about more than just being a good lawyer** - Client service excellence is about so much more than just great technical abilities; it is about exhibiting emotional intelligence, which is priceless to clients. There is no other way to cultivate successful client relationships than to inspire trust, and the most effective way to do so is to build a meaningful foundation by exhibiting a high EQ. As professional services expert David Maister so aptly stated, *"Ultimately, hiring a lawyer is about confidence and trust. It is an emotional act."*

Business Development, Deconstructed

For many professionals in service-based industries, especially those of us who have built our careers on our expertise, excellence and word-of-mouth referrals, it can feel awkward or even insincere to think of spending time and energy developing our business. Many of us inherit limiting beliefs, whether from our parents, colleagues or mentors, that real professionals just keep their heads down and do great work, that marketing is fluff, and that business and clients will inevitably come our way if we are good enough at what we do.

The truth is that doing excellent work is essential, but it is not the whole picture. In today's economy, where clients have more options, information and expectations than ever before, we cannot afford to treat business development as an afterthought. If we want to create sustainable, impactful and fulfilling careers, companies and communities, then business development must become a mindset and a way of life, not just another thing to do after we have done everything else on our task list.

Debunking Business Development Myths

There are a number of myths that keep many talented professionals from fully embracing business development:

Myth: Business development is just marketing fluff.
Truth: Business development is strategic, relevant and invaluable. The best in the business are constantly refining how they connect, serve and grow with others.

Myth: Business development is for people who do not have real work to do.

Truth: Business development is what high-performing professionals do to ensure they *have* work in the first place.

Myth: You are either born with business development skills or not.
Truth: Like leadership, business development is learned, practiced and refined, evolving over time.

Myth: If you are good at your job, clients will come.
Truth: This may be true to an extent, but it is foolish to bet your business on it. The market does not owe us anything.

Know Yourself (and What You're Selling)

At the heart of any powerful business development strategy is clarity. You must first understand who you are, what you are offering and why it matters. If you do not know the value of what you bring to the table, or tend to downplay or overinflate your offerings, your message will fall flat, or even worse, be disingenuous.

This clarity is not about packaging yourself in a flashy way or portraying a version of yourself that you think the market wants. It is about aligning what differentiates you, your capabilities, passions and integrity with the needs of the people you serve. When you know what you do well and who you want to help, you stop trying to be everything to everyone, which is where your real power lies.

Your Audience is Listening—Are You Speaking Their Language?

Once you have gotten honest about your value, the next step is understanding your audience. What are they struggling with? What keeps them up at night? Where are their pressure points? What would make their lives or work easier, better and more joyful?

Business development begins with robust listening. When we stay curious about the needs, desires and behaviors of the people we want to serve, we build connection and relevance which, in the business world, is powerful currency. No amount of charisma or clever branding will save a service offering that is disconnected from the problems clients are actually trying to solve.

So before you jump into your next pitch, take a step back and ask yourself: "Is what I'm offering something my potential clients actually want, or just something I want to sell?"

Relationships First. Always.

What is the biggest myth in business development? That it is all about cold calls, boondoggles and forcing your way into conversations and situations. Nothing could be further from the truth. At its core, business development is about building relationships - authentic, mutual, human connections. We do business with people we know, like and trust. That's not fluff, it's neuroscience.

Your most powerful business development asset is your ability to build genuine connections, follow up consistently, stay top of mind without being annoying, and offer value without expectation. Whether you are meeting someone virtually, volunteering in your community, speaking on a panel or running into a potential client at the grocery store, every interaction is an opportunity to plant a seed. Not every seed will grow, but some will become partnerships, clients, referrals, collaborations, and even lifelong friends.

Face Time Still Matters

Yes, we live in a digital world. Video calls, texts, emails and social media are all important. But we should not underestimate the power of real, face-to-face connection. There is simply no substitute for being in the room, sitting across from someone, making eye contact and having a conversation.

When the opportunity presents itself to meet in person, seize it - even if your calendar is packed and it requires extra effort. That experience could be a game-changer. Business gets done when people feel seen, heard and understood, and that is much easier to do when we are physically present.

Your Reputation Is Your Brand

Whether we like it or not, people talk about us. While some of the content may be out of our control, a lot of it isn't. Clients and colleagues make referrals for people they trust, and recommend those who show up, follow through and do great work. Your brand is your reputation. It is what people think when they hear your name. It is how you show up in rooms where decisions are made, even when you are not in them. Every email you send, every deadline you meet (or miss), every social media post you make, and every handshake contributes to your personal brand. Are you known for being thoughtful? Consistent? Innovative? Reliable? That is why being a genuinely excellent professional is still the best business development strategy there is.

Strategic, Not Random

Business development is not a scattershot of lunch meetings and LinkedIn posts. It is a disciplined, intentional effort to build a business that aligns with your vision, values and goals. Stop committing random acts of marketing. Instead, plan, plan, plan - identify your targets, invest in meaningful connections, and be willing to play the long game. It is a well-known statistic that it may take 8 to 10 thoughtful interactions before a lead converts to a client. That is not failure, it's reality. Remember, be strategic, persistent and patient.

Learn, Adapt, Repeat

No two professionals have the same business development style. Some shine on stage, while others are brilliant one-on-one. Some love to write, while others love to teach. The key is to find what works for *you,* hone it, refine it, and evolve over time.

Seek out mentors. Watch what the truly successful rainmakers do. Experiment. And remember: just because someone else's strategy works for them, does not mean it will work for you. You are not trying to be a carbon copy of someone else; you are trying to be the best version of yourself, amplified.

From David's perspective:

"This is true whether you work in a law firm or in-house, and applies in non-legal business settings as well. People need to know me, they need to like me, and they need to trust me, or they will not work with me. 'Like' does not necessarily mean you must be social friends, though that is sometimes a bonus. It means that people need to be comfortable enough with you that they will talk with you and develop a level of trust so that they will want to work with you as their lawyer."

Speak Your Power—In 30 Seconds or Less

The elevator speech is one of the most overlooked tools in business development. When someone asks what you do, can you answer clearly, compellingly and concisely? Are you able to communicate not just your job title but also your value, your passion and your unique angle?

This really matters. In a world where attention spans are getting shorter by the day, the ability to articulate who you are, how you help others and what differentiates you on the spot is business development gold. A great elevator pitch is not a one-size-fits-all script. It is a living, breathing, evolving introduction to you and your brand, tailored to the moment, the target and the opportunity.

Be patient with yourself through the process of writing, rewriting and honing your elevator speech. Mark Twain once said, *"If you want me to give you a two-hour presentation, I am ready today. If you only want a five-*

minute speech, it will take me two weeks to prepare." There is a lot of truth to that.

Be Genuine and Generous

Business development is not about ego. It is about evolution. When we treat it as an act of service, not just for our business but for our community, we will all succeed. At the end of the day, the most powerful form of business development is generosity, integrity and a desire to provide first-rate service to your clients and colleagues. When you lift others up, share your knowledge, and connect people simply because you can, you build an authentic brand that people trust. You become the kind of professional others want to work with, recommend and support.

Law Firms

In an ideal world, the size of a law firm would not meaningfully impact the type of legal service someone would receive. Unfortunately, we do not live in an ideal world, and there are only so many hours in a day. Law firms, like all businesses, only have a certain amount of resources. The question really becomes: What do legal services look like across different sizes of firms? Understandably, smaller firms have fewer people and so, when you are talking about the kind of experience those firms bring to the table, they can usually offer a deep bench in only one or few areas. But when it comes to having a multitude of practice areas with a deep bench or expansive geography, you do not generally see that with small firms, just because they do not have the necessary infrastructure. When it comes to administrative resources, they do not generally offer what larger firms do when it comes to things like marketing, professional development, training, pro bono and so forth. Large firms, on the other hand, are often known for a number of practice areas. Along with the cache of their names comes a multitude of disciplines, a deep bench, as well as expansive geography.

You can get first-rate quality legal services from both small and large firms. It really depends on the nature of the matter and the substantive experience you are looking for from your lawyer. It is not as simple as rates and fees. Large firms may develop certain efficiencies and may actually be less expensive than smaller firms on a given matter, and the reverse can also be true.

Some small firm lawyers and sole practitioners started out their careers in large firms, and they may offer the same level of subject matter expertise that you would find in bigger firms, so you can get comparable quality of legal service. If you have national or global matters, a large firm may have an advantage because they have a larger geographic footprint.

Ultimately, it comes down to the sophistication necessary for the matter, how important and how valuable the matter is to the company, and the relationship with outside counsel.

Depending on the type of matter - and whether it is a short-term or a long-term project, and if you are looking for an attorney who is going to be your advisor, particularly on a longer-term basis - it is important to look at potential candidates both as an attorney and a person. Are you able to develop that rapport? What do they bring to the table, and what does their firm offer?

Client needs and demands have significantly shifted over the past few years. There are several reasons for this, including the globalization of business, the ever-increasing frequency with which technology evolves, and geographical fluctuations, all of which have forever changed the landscape of the legal profession. As a result, law firms have had to significantly adapt their business models to survive. There are some firms willing to take risks with visionary approaches and, as a result, have been able to thrive. As law firms continue to evolve, there is recognition that in order to survive, they must figure out who they are and what meaningfully differentiates them from others in the marketplace.

As businesses become more international in scope, many firms have significantly increased in size and geographic footprint and have crossed the global threshold. Some firms have also expanded their service offerings to more closely mirror their client's needs. As a result of the continued volatility in demand for outside legal services, the workforce has been impacted. This drives law firms and law departments to become more nimble and adaptable to changes in the market. The overall legal environment is more competitive with much more of an emphasis on value-based billing and a move away from the billable hour. As a result, firms have been forced to be much more accommodating and creative for their clients than they have been in the past.

How to Tell the Differences Between Law Firms

At first blush, firms may seem very similar to each other. However, when you take a closer look, you realize that they each have differentiators. A firm's personality is driven by its people and senior management. If they are entrepreneurial, innovative and proactive, the firm's identity and direction will look a lot different than a firm that prefers the status quo, resists change and is reactive. A firm's spirit drives many characteristics, including its geographic footprint, its size, its practice offerings and specialties. Also key is how it positions itself in the marketplace and what its mission is – no one firm can be everything to everybody, and those which recognize and embrace their differentiators as a strength and opportunity are more likely to thrive in the long term.

From David's perspective:

"Two of the most important things I look for in outside counsel are quality of client service and creativity. Expertise in particular substantive areas is critical but that is not really the distinguishing factor today. Firms differentiate themselves by demonstrating an entrepreneurial and proactive spirit and culture. Firms can no longer rest on their laurels, but must be out in front creatively, suggesting solutions, demonstrating both the ability and willingness to collaborate with me to best achieve my goals and, when necessary, helping me to find and articulate those goals.

Client service is also critical. That includes timely responsiveness, taking the time to learn my needs and desired outcomes and as much as possible about my company. The ability to properly staff a matter is part of this, as building the right team is more than mere substantive expertise. Another important component is having a strong relationship partner, someone who is responsible for the overall relationship, who knows me and my company, and is my go-to person, no matter what the matter or issue may be."

The Biggest Benefit of Law Firms for In-House Counsel

Law firms can provide a multitude of benefits to in-house counsel. Those benefits which stand out may vary depending on the focus with any given engagement. A large law firm can serve as a one-stop shop capable of handling many or all of a client's needs across disciplines and geographies, which in turn can create tremendous efficiencies in terms of consistency, quality, speed and overall value. This is a tremendous benefit because it eliminates the need to train new counsel about a company every time an issue arises in a different location. It also means fewer outside firms to manage and fewer bills to review, which is very meaningful to in-house lawyers.

Large firms generally have strong depth and sophistication in various practice areas that make them ideal for a given matter or portfolio of work within those specialties. They also have a large bench of talent, which can be particularly valuable in certain situations. For example, if an acquisition requires due diligence and closing to be completed within a very tight window, a large firm may be ideal because it has the substantive experience, a bench of lawyers, and the support staff and facilities necessary to meet the client's needs.

There are a number of advantages when it comes to working at a large law firm. They are generally known for the great training they provide their lawyers. They are also known for their ability to provide a significant depth and breadth of talent across many different practice areas and geographies. Moreover, given the sheer number of attorneys that work at these firms, clients appreciate being able to access numerous attorneys with similar skillsets, particularly if their lead lawyer is unavailable. As a result, there are certain types of matters (e.g., "bet the company" litigation) that will often go to large firms. There are also certain practice areas that may only make sense within a large firm, because of the nature of its client base, its geographic footprint and the synergies that those areas provide with the firm's other service offerings.

Our profession continues to undergo a transformative metamorphosis, particularly with respect to globalization, consolidation and convergence. This evolution is directly driven by changes which many clients are experiencing, particularly with respect to where, how and with whom they are doing business. For such companies, a large law firm and, in particular, a global firm may be best positioned to service their legal needs.

When in-house counsel seek legal representation, they are hiring both the lawyers and the law firm. Their relative importance is highly dependent on the specific circumstances. Christina explains, *"In my experience, clients want to feel a certain affinity for their relationship partner and trust them in order for the engagement to be truly successful."* That partner is often the first person who a client meets from the firm and will often be the one to introduce that client to the firm's capabilities and to those attorneys whose subject matter capabilities align with the client's legal needs. It is important for the client to both like and respect the partner who serves in this role, since they will give the client the necessary comfort to invest more time and resources into the overall relationship.

A client's experience is shaped so much by the relationship partner and their lawyering skills, demeanor, responsiveness and ability to create effective teams across whatever disciplines the client's legal needs may dictate. While in many ways relationship partners are only as good as the team with whom they work, if they are truly effective, they will successfully serve not only as the lead lawyer for the relationship, but also as the client's trusted advisor and confidante.

From David's perspective:

"When I need outside counsel, the first consideration is always going to be finding subject matter knowledge that matches my needs. There are times when I have a relationship with a lawyer or I have received a referral to a particular lawyer because of his or her skillset. The particular firm for whom that lawyer works may not matter so much initially. However, a strong relationship partner will expand the relationship beyond the initial

engagement so that, going forward, I will begin working with the firm for multiple matters, in multiple practice areas, still maintaining strong ties with the relationship partner. There are other times when I specifically want a big firm, such as in a mergers and acquisitions (M&A) scenario, or because of the nature of the matter or the firm's reputation in a given area, and I want the goodwill associated with that firm for a particular reason. In those cases, I am hiring the firm first, rather than the particular lawyer."

The Future of Law Firms

Trends fluctuate, based on any number of factors, including the global economy and various geopolitical factors. We anticipate continued consolidation in the legal market, which will ultimately drive the evolution of more global firms. We will see more mergers, and some firms are going to end up getting bigger. There will be some that will dissolve or be reborn into different organizations. That being said, we will also continue seeing smaller firms and sole practitioners. When it comes to the success of a law firm, it is ultimately driven by the individuals in those firms. Being diligent and proactive is really important, not only when it comes to your clients but also in running the business. You have to be nimble and able to react quickly to your client's needs and to determine what direction the marketplace is driving your business.

Alternative fee arrangements are increasingly the norm, with less reliance on the billable hour. We expect firms will continue to evolve with fewer equity partners and more of a traditional pyramid shape. David explains, *"I think there will be fewer partners and more non-partner track attorneys, such as staff attorneys and counsel."*

In terms of the future of leadership, law firms need to thread a delicate needle, between rewarding its most successful rainmakers in meaningful ways while at the same time ensuring that people who have a knack and a talent for leadership are also rewarded. It takes a special kind of person to lead a professional services firm. Sometimes the skills required to build a big book of business do not necessarily translate into being a strong leader.

Going Global

Law Firms and Legal Departments as Global Organizations

Both law firms and legal departments are invaluable partners in addressing legal and business issues. Even if a business' operations are primarily domestic in scope, given the global nature of the economy, the marketplace, politics and technological interconnectivity, every business has a ripple effect on others, and vice versa. It is inevitable that customers, legal and business issues, and problem-solving processes and solutions, each have an international reach.

We live in a global economy. This means that all businesses and their lawyers must be where their clients are, both substantively and geographically, and able to think multi-nationally, even if the business only operates locally.

The Challenges of Being a Global Organization

One of the biggest challenges is in striking a delicate balance among a variety of competing interests, all of which are important to the long-term success of an organization. This includes reaching an optimal solution to the legal and business issues which arise, particularly where the consequences are international in scope. It is also a challenge to stay current, relevant and competitive in each of the financial centers across the world. Seamless and open communication with your team members and clients across the globe is vital. You must also be proactive, forward-thinking, innovative and a leader, rather than being reactive and a follower.

Another major challenge is knowing the laws, customs and culture of other countries in which you are doing business. Culture impacts business, and you must be able to negotiate and bridge any differences successfully in order to have a global practice. These challenges include navigating language and time zone differences, as well as any differences in problem-solving approaches and deal and negotiation cadences.

The Necessary Skills to Go Global

Lawyers with a successful global practice are, first and foremost, great substantive lawyers with a strong business sense and excellent interpersonal skills. They are open-minded and able to appreciate legal and business issues from a variety of angles. They also have a working understanding and sensitivity to other cultures, customs and perspectives. To the extent that there is a knowledge gap, they are willing to learn through work projects, and they also study, travel and seek advice from others with such experience. In addition, they are collaborative, a team player and have an understanding that legal and business decisions in today's global environment will often have a ripple effect beyond the matter at hand, and analyze issues from that perspective as well.

Flexibility and patience are also important. You cannot be too set in your ways, because your counterpart across the globe likely sees things differently. You need to compromise to accomplish your goals. Be mindful of your limitations and retain experienced counsel to help you navigate those areas in which you may not have the requisite skills or knowledge. While you can always learn technical details and applicable law, working successfully with people from different countries, cultures and world views requires a skillset that is as much people-oriented as it is substantive.

Bridging Generations Together for Greater Success

There are now several generations of professionals who are providing and purchasing legal services. Each generation often sees the world a bit differently from the others, and these points of view are often shaped by an individual's personal and professional experiences as well as the world events that have defined their generations. In addition, generations are often characterized by how they prioritize professional and personal responsibilities and where they draw certain boundaries. There are often other distinguishing characteristics, such as different problem-solving strategies, ways to intake and process information and to manage tasks, as well as communication and working styles. There are important differences across generations, and it is essential to bridge any that may exist.

Today's workplace encompasses many different generations, each of which needs to join efforts with the others to bridge their different work and communication styles. The hope is that younger generations who are accustomed to communicating virtually will learn the value and importance of face-to-face interaction, and that older generations will see the value in allowing professionals to work remotely and increased collaboration through the use of technology.

Both Baby Boomers and Gen Xers have seen many changes in the way law is practiced, especially due to the impact of technology that did not exist when they began practicing. Younger generations typically have different communication and working styles than older generations, having grown up with technology and social media. These changes present opportunities wherein both generations can learn from each other, such as the importance of balancing office time with the desire to work remotely.

There has also been an increased focus on mentoring. While it has long been the case that younger attorneys learn from experienced lawyers, mentoring has become a higher priority and more purposeful practice. Mentoring is a two-way street, exposing both mentor and mentee to new ideas and styles, thereby building bridges across generations.

The Evolution of Multigenerational Issues

The issues we face with a multigenerational workforce are becoming more front and center over time. Today's younger generations will gain more experience and will move up the professional ladder with greater responsibility in the next few years. It is at these career inflection points when it becomes even more critical to bridge whatever gaps may exist across generations. This will require a certain amount of awareness, empathy and desire on everyone's part to accomplish this goal. The increased focus on developing one's emotional intelligence in recent years will become even more important over time, and those who have not yet done so will need to harness these qualities within themselves so that they do not get left behind.

How to Effectively Engage Across Generations

Effective engagement includes meaningfully communicating and understanding others. Successful communication involves timely articulating your point of view, needs and desires, as well as actively listening to those of others, and being able to act upon that knowledge accordingly. It is important to achieve that mutual understanding and to take proactive steps to learn more about others if you find that there is a communication disconnect. The ultimate objective is to strike a balance that enables everyone to leverage their similarities, as well as bridging any differences which may exist across generations and to channel them into sound decision-making and collaborative teamwork. Putting yourself in another's shoes may sound cliché, but it is one of the most powerful steps you can take to more effectively understand others.

When generations initially meet in the workplace, their differences may appear quite stark, and the first reaction may be suspicion and rejection of the other's way of doing things. Professionals, like businesses, need to evolve, adapt and grow to remain relevant. Different generations need to learn to hear one another and work toward common goals. There is value in each generation's different ways of doing things. People must learn to collaborate, adapt and evolve. What initially seems foreign or cumbersome may quickly become easy and comfortable, and perhaps even better or more efficient. Learning goes both ways, and no generation has a monopoly on the best way to do things. Don't knock it until you try it.

The Impacts of a Multigenerational Workforce

Multiple generations can have different ideas about how to problem solve and approach issues, as well as distinct points of view. These distinctions can bring new, fresh energy into the environment that can help spark creativity. While working styles may not align, particularly if decades separate the generations, these differences can be leveraged into figuring out the optimal ways to get things done which incorporate both the old and the new. Having different generations in the workplace also presents a form of diversity which is critically important to the health of the organization.

While multi-generational workforces may sometimes create friction, it is important to smooth it out. If it persists, it can create a lack of fresh ideas, a lack of innovation, and irrelevancy. We all know the world is constantly evolving. We need multigenerational workforces not only to keep pace, but to excel. Generational gaps, whether from generations not communicating well with each other or because certain generations are missing in your workplace, can bring about these issues. Having multiple generations present and working together is an important form of inclusion that helps an organization succeed.

How to Best Bridge and Leverage Generational Differences in the Workplace

The only way to truly tackle these issues and to effectively leverage the positive aspects of generational differences is to acknowledge when the tension exists and figure out where the heart of the discord lies. Usually, it signals the need for improved communication among team members, and to create an environment in which people are not only speaking freely about their views and concerns, but they are also listening so that they can understand other approaches and viewpoints. It is essential for leadership to foster a collaborative environment with patience and transparency as a foundation, which will lead to future breakthroughs.

There are many ways to bridge this gap. For example, ensure that your workplace employs individuals from multiple generations and that they work together in teams, and not in isolation. If that is not possible, then collaborate with people from generations different from your own outside of your job. Solicit ideas and contributions from those of other generations, not just your own. Team building and training exercises, especially with a trained moderator, can help tremendously. Learn the different needs and working styles, and build ways to bridge them. Human resources teams can lead a workshop in personality types and then discuss the different skills and styles of communication. Develop systems to provide feedback and mentoring for all of your employees.

It is also important to maintain a positive attitude. There is much to learn and teach when there are different generations represented in the workplace, as well as opportunities to pay it forward that otherwise may not exist. Just remember these issues have been around since time immemorial. Discard preconceived notions that your way is necessarily the right way, and listen to new ideas, and be open to new approaches. Embrace change - "that's how we've always done it" is not the way to approach problem-solving. Mentoring and contributing in the workplace is best done when all are welcoming and willing to engage.

Mentoring and Executive Coaching

As the business world continues to be extraordinarily competitive, it is more important than ever for professionals to be at the top of their game. A professional's performance is now measured by much more than just how good they are technically. Indeed, clients evaluate and hire based on many other, more subjective characteristics. However, these skills are not always taught in school, and their importance is often undervalued during a professional's formative years. Yet these are the very attributes that differentiate merely solid performers from high performers - the good from the great.

One key ingredient to professional success is powerful mentoring relationships. These partnerships enable a mentor and a protégé to meaningfully collaborate toward achieving specific, well-defined career and personal goals. Mentoring can take a variety of forms, both formal and informal, and is free of gender, racial, ethnic and age restrictions.

Developing a Circle of Trusted Peers

There are organizations that are created for this very purpose — to provide membership opportunities to professionals who wish to formally become part of such a circle. But for those who wish to develop this type of circle more organically, it requires a combination of focus, strategy and serendipity. Focus comes from thinking carefully about what you are looking to accomplish professionally through a peer circle, and being determined and willing to put in the hard work to get there. You also need to be strategic in figuring out how best to get there and not leaving fulfillment of your goals to chance. Serendipity often factors in when, for example, you see that old acquaintance who happens to know someone you really want to meet, or by landing a speaking opportunity with a trade association that has many representatives from companies with whom you would like to do business. But remember — you have to be alert and open-minded to notice when serendipity is working its magic in your life.

From David's Perspective:

"The most significant trade group in my career has been the Association of Corporate Counsel (ACC). I joined when I first went in-house in 1999, primarily for the educational and substantive resources. I remain active because of the professional and personal relationships I have made. I am able to bounce not only substantive legal questions off of my contacts, but to also obtain career and situational advice. Volunteering with not-for-profits is another avenue that can help develop a circle of trusted peers and also provides an opportunity to learn from others outside your specific profession."

What is Peer Mentoring?

Peer mentoring means looking to contemporaries, both at work and elsewhere, to provide you with the support, guidance, perspective and assistance you need to develop professionally. Just as important, peer mentoring provides you with the opportunity to fill that role for others as well. As you get further in your career, it often becomes more difficult to find what we call the more traditional mentors - those who are "older and wiser" and with whom the traditional lines of teacher and student are clearly drawn.

Peer mentoring provides an opportunity for continued growth for each of us, albeit in a context that recognizes our depth and breadth of experience, while at the same time acknowledging the importance of learning. You can glean a tremendous amount by having conversations with different business leaders and others within your company, and you can learn at least as much simply by observing the way they conduct themselves in different situations and audiences.

While sharing substantive professional expertise is an important part of mentoring, the emotional intelligence of both the mentor and mentee is critical to the overall success of the mentoring dynamic. The most effective mentoring draws upon the mentor's ability to identify his or her own emotions and those of others, manage both sets of emotions, motivate oneself and others, and manage the overall mentoring relationship. The mentee must likewise exhibit these types of soft skills to maximize the relationship's effectiveness.

Advantages of Peer Mentoring

There is a lot of wisdom and guidance that we can all gather from those around us. Getting this type of coaching from others can be particularly helpful when they have encountered similar situations, successes and obstacles, and when those experiences are at least somewhat contemporaneous with ours. There are significant advantages to sharing these types of stories and anecdotes with peers both within and outside of our organization. There is also the intel gathering aspect to peer mentoring, which includes learning helpful information about other businesses. Finally, peer mentoring is a terrific exercise in building relationships and can often lead to meaningful networking.

In order to be the best we can be in all aspects of our lives, we must constantly strive to learn and to better our skills, both substantively and interpersonally. Gaining insights from your professional colleagues is one of the best ways to accomplish this, and to remain current with what is happening within your organization and your industry.

How To Be an Effective Mentor

Effective mentors have a number of key personal attributes. These include being authentic, candid, non-judgmental, empathetic, committed, inspirational, positive and successful. Mentoring is a form of supportive coaching; rather than focusing on a mentee's weaknesses, mentors should focus on enabling the mentee's strengths to foster growth and to see the magic in themselves.

At the outset, mentors should choose their mentees wisely and set the tone of the relationship to ensure that there is alignment of attitudes, goals and expectations. Both must speak the same language and, since the most effective coaching styles differ from person to person, mentors must discern which method will work best for the mentee. There should be agreement up front as to how the success or failure of the mentoring relationship will be measured. In addition, a dynamic and communicative environment must be created where feedback is both openly offered and willingly received. Confidentiality is a critical part of developing and maintaining mutual trust.

Mentors should provide concrete, practical tips on successfully navigating through various types of substantive and political issues within the mentee's organization. Mentors serve as sounding boards, and their candor is particularly important, especially with the more delicate issues facing the mentee. In addition to sharing specific tips and guidance, mentors should share war stories, which often provide the most memorable teaching. Indeed, sometimes the best lessons that mentors can impart are about their failures and what they learned as a result, rather than their successes.

As the relationship develops, mentors should remember that the ultimate goal is to enable the mentee to flourish and grow to their full potential, whatever that may be, even if the mentee ultimately takes a very different path than the mentor. Mentors must remain mindful that these relationships are not meant to last forever. In fact, some of the most effective mentoring occurs under a fixed timeline of limited duration, which helps ensure that the mentor and mentee stay focused on the specific goals of the partnership. Mentors should be sensitive to signals as to when the relationship has run its course and should carefully determine how best to wind it down in a timely, constructive and thoughtful way.

How To Be a Successful Mentee

A successful mentee is appreciative, courageous, eager to learn, flexible, open-minded, resilient and self-confident. They have a clear vision of what they hope to achieve and are likewise discerning in choosing their mentor. They realize that some of the best mentoring relationships are ones that develop organically and informally, and are open to such experiences. Mentees should be willing to step outside their comfort zone and are well-served to seek experiences from a wide variety of people, including ones with whom they have little in common but who nevertheless have much to teach. In fact, cultivating a number of mentoring relationships over time is an invaluable way to learn and share a variety of perspectives and styles.

Mentees should be active participants in the mentoring partnership; the dynamic should be one of both give and take. They should be willing to break old habits and develop new ones by taking the coaching and working diligently to ensure that they are actively integrating the mentor's advice into their lives. Mentors can provide mentees with a number of benefits, including access to their professional contacts, and mentees should understand the importance and value of developing this aspect of the relationship. They should also be mindful that mentoring relationships are just one component of an effective professional development strategy, and mentees should contemporaneously seek other types of opportunities by which they can learn and grow.

Finally, mentees should show appreciation for their mentor's generosity and should remember the importance of "paying it forward" by sharing their knowledge and experiences with other professionals.

While mentoring requires a significant commitment of time and resources by both mentor and mentee, it provides an effective, meaningful way to assist professionals in their career advancement. This investment is also a fundamental part of an organization's leadership development and succession planning; it is invaluable in positioning it for future success.

Exploring Executive Coaching

There are a variety of ways that professionals can effectively drive self-improvement and success. On-the-job training and mentoring are two primary development techniques. However, it becomes increasingly difficult to continue growing at a steep trajectory throughout one's career solely relying on these methods. One must often look to other, more creative ways to hone the necessary skills to become better professionals, role models and people. Executive coaching provides one such mechanism. It has long been used by organizations in developing their high-level executives and individuals being groomed for those positions. It is a form of professional development and mentoring which provides a framework and context within which professionals can assess where they are and where they are headed.

Executive coaching performs a number of valuable functions. It helps you to prioritize what is important to you, develop a strategy for reaching your goals, and implement an action plan using that strategy. Coaches take you from theory into the real world and help you identify your strengths, weaknesses, self-limiting behaviors and blind spots. They give you honest, real-time feedback and provide accountability, support and candor in a way that most other people cannot. Coaches see you in the same way others see you, and one of the core aspects of the relationship is teaching you that, for better or worse, other people's perceptions of you often drive your experience in the world.

Coaches ask powerful questions designed to elicit answers that will fundamentally impact the coaching process. The relationship must be built on trust and confidentiality - without them, it will fail. As Harvard Business School Professor Thomas Delong states, *"Coaches are truth speakers - they tell you what you need to hear, not necessarily what you want to hear."* This is critically important, particularly as you grow into a more seasoned professional, since it becomes increasingly difficult to obtain this information from those with whom you work, particularly when they are people who report to you. Coaches also function as good sounding boards and are committed to your success, no matter how you choose to define it.

It is important to understand what coaching is not. First, it is not a substitute for therapy or other forms of treatment. Sometimes there are issues that need to be addressed by certain types of trained professionals such as psychiatrists or doctors, not by coaches. Depending on your specific needs, coaching can actually do more harm than good if you are not receiving the appropriate help you need. In addition, coaching does not provide a quick fix to your issues and problems. Rather, it is a process of self-discovery and self-development and takes time to unfold.

If a coach is promising quick, easy answers with little or no effort on your part, you should carefully consider whether the coach is truly qualified. You must also be open to constructive criticism, to follow the process wherever it may lead you and to change your attitudes, habits and behaviors, particularly when they are self-defeating or destructive. You should bring your goals and desires to the process, rather than expecting your coach to tell you what they should be. Good coaches are not focused on their own agenda, or on that of the organization paying for their services. Instead, they only think about you and what you are trying to accomplish. In addition, coaching is not meant to dwell on the past. Although it can be helpful in figuring out what has and has not worked for you, coaching should be focused on creating a present and future that you want.

Picking the right coach is critical to a successful experience. There are many who claim a great track record and proven techniques. Unfortunately, it is often difficult to discern whether this is actually the case until you start working with one. Like all of us, they each have their strengths and weaknesses, some of which may or may not complement your own. For this reason, it is often better to start by speaking with individuals you know who have successfully worked with executive coaches, who can provide you with some insight into the process and who may be able to give you good referrals. It is important to then interview those coaches whom you are considering and to get a clear idea of their personalities, working style, what they envision for your coaching experience, and the types of professionals with whom they typically work. You need to both like and respect your coach. Otherwise, they are unlikely to get to know you in the way that is necessary for the process to truly work.

Finally, you need to figure out your budget and what type of coach you can afford. It is important to consider the frequency with which you intend to meet with your coach as well as the likely overall duration of the process. You should budget for some extra sessions in case unexpected issues come up requiring additional sessions. While working with a coach may stretch your budget, the benefits are often dramatic, long-lasting and well worth the investment. It is a truly transformative experience that invokes positive changes in the way you see your career and life, and the way that others see you.

Change Management

Change management is the process by which an organization and its members transition from one place or state to another. Given how quickly the professional landscape continues to evolve, businesses must be nimble and respond in kind. Change management provides a framework by which we can work through necessary transitions in such a way so that we are able to do what needs to be done while, at the same time, providing our colleagues with the necessary tools to understand and embrace the change and help push it forward. Without such methodologies, change can be a very difficult proposition.

Change management can also be thought of as a way of driving the people side of change to achieve a desired outcome. When done well, change management engages people and enables them to feel invested in the change process, incentivizing all to work toward a common objective. It is not a standalone process for designing business solutions, nor is it a process improvement plan. Rather, change management provides the framework for instituting organizational change with the major focus being on people and bringing about a smooth transition. The importance of change management lies in careful planning and frequent, effective communication, thus becoming the key to ensuring long-term, lasting success.

Why Change Management can be Challenging for Lawyers

When you look at the typical personality profile for lawyers, there is an underlying theme that emerges - skepticism and resistance to change. Much of this is born of being risk-averse by nature, which enables lawyers to be good at what they do - advising clients on how best to protect themselves and to mitigate risk. Lawyers are also analytical by nature, and they require a lot of facts and information before evaluating a particular proposal.

There are ways for leaders to leverage these qualities among their constituencies so as to effectively garner support. However, it requires hard work, patience and transparency along the way. It also means that leaders need to check their egos at the door and understand that there is tremendous value in having their team members ask questions and challenge their thinking. This helps ensure that they will reach an optimal result with their decision-making and that there will be buy-in with whatever change they are trying to implement.

Resistance to change is normal for most, especially lawyers. It is difficult and creates uncertainty. By providing lawyers with a specified framework for achieving a desired outcome, it becomes much easier for them to get on board and embrace the change. Lawyers are also uniquely suited to help lead that change because they are adept at asking the right questions and challenging conventional ways of thinking. This is enhanced if they have built up their reputations as trusted advisors and valued team members.

How to Successfully Drive Change in Your Organization

The first step in driving change is recognizing that change is needed. You must develop a clear vision of the type of change that is required, and you then need to create a roadmap for getting from where you are to where you want to be. This can be tricky, since it involves a series of short and long-term steps. You should develop a series of contingency plans to address the various ways your plan may play out. You also need to clearly communicate your strategy for change so that you can rally the necessary support. As part of that, it is important to consider how the message of change will be received by your various constituencies and tailor the message accordingly depending on your audience. You also need to carefully consider the impact change will have on the culture of your organization. It most certainly will be at the forefront of everyone's minds, and you must demonstrate that you have carefully thought it through.

In-house lawyers, with relationships both within and outside the legal department, can also help lead change in their companies. It is important to help ensure alignment of the organizational values, people and behaviors. In-house attorneys can help their business colleagues to make the case for change by helping develop a formal plan before it is launched, one that not only explains the purpose and goals but that also includes how to communicate the plan and explain what happens to their jobs, their careers, their roles in the company and the business going forward. They can also help prepare for the unexpected. Nothing ever goes as planned and, as lawyers, we are well-equipped to consider in advance how to handle the unexpected and help our colleagues to do the same.

CRISIS MANAGEMENT

A crisis is an issue that arises that is of great significance to an individual or an organization, such as a high-stakes matter. Crises can come in all shapes and sizes. They are sometimes easy to spot, but other times, they are more insidious. Clients may not realize a situation is even a crisis until it has reached fever pitch, which often makes it more difficult and costly to resolve.

There are crises which are existential threats to organizations, such as a natural disaster, the loss of a key leader or a data breach. But there are also crises that simply arise in the daily functioning of a business, such as discrimination claims or employee injuries. Crisis management is not just about navigating and managing through such events; it is also about proactive planning and managing on a daily basis to prevent crises before they happen, and to minimize their impact when they occur.

From Christina's perspective:

"I have partnered with numerous clients in crisis management over my career. For example, a few of my life sciences clients have experienced crises when a regulatory agency has rejected a proposed brand name a few weeks before a product's expected launch date. Postponing a drug launch even for a few days can cost a company many millions of dollars. When in this situation, we work with clients to help them conduct expedited global risk assessments for alternate brands until they find a substitute.

I also regularly assist clients with crises outside of my practice area. For example, I had a client who was encountering difficulties with a labor union engaging in activities intended to profoundly disrupt my client's business and customer relationships. The initial grievance seemed to be primarily based in violations of intellectual property law, but it became evident the situation required the assistance of my labor and employment colleagues who specialize in addressing these types of union issues. This is one of the many advantages of being at a general practice firm; I can tap into the expertise of attorneys outside of my practice area to deliver solutions to clients in crisis."

From David's perspective:

"One crisis I dealt with in a previous in-house position was when I learned our largest customer was encouraging our employees to leave us to work at a competing company. We assembled a team to develop defensive and offensive plans, and I delivered a letter to the customer declaring them in breach of contract. The next day, the court granted a temporary restraining order (TRO), including a key provision that prevented the customer from hiring away our employees during the TRO - giving us breathing room to remain in business and reach an amicable settlement.

I generally employ one or more of the following forms of crisis management: (1) Immediately investigate an appropriate way to address the situation or behavior; and (2) Create and maintain a culture of open communication and respect for both people and processes at all levels. By identifying a crisis early and investigating quickly, most cases can be resolved with hurt feelings ameliorated, jobs saved and an existential crisis averted."

Navigating a Client Crisis

Crises can be difficult to identify. Sometimes people confuse an urgent matter with a crisis when it does not warrant the same level of significance; at other times, a real crisis may not be treated with the proper level of attention, at least not right away. Thus, it is important to do what you can to properly identify an issue for what it is - crisis or not - as quickly as possible. Moreover, it is helpful for organizations to consider whether there are costly and disruptive situations that come up on a regular basis. If that is the case, you should help your clients create a protocol for addressing those issues and ensure your team is well-equipped to handle crises when they arise. It is imperative that the crisis management team remains calm, even under the most difficult of circumstances, and receives the proper training so it is properly prepared.

It is also important to cultivate a culture where employees feel a sense of ownership and the freedom to speak up and help fix mistakes or situations. In such an environment, mistakes are less likely to grow into problems that can quickly become full-blown crises. Documentation is another key to avoiding crises - for example, processes and procedures that can help a company get back on its feet after disaster strikes or to defend itself against litigation.

Navigating Uncertainty

While the topic of navigating uncertainty is one that many of us have experienced in one way or another, it became a serious issue affecting the entire world in early 2020 with the COVID-19 pandemic, lockdown, and shelter-in-place orders across the country.

Uncertainty in the Workplace

Uncertainty is not clearly defined, and can relate to any number of things. Uncertainty comes in all forms. It can mean a lack of confidence. Will I get this job? Will I win this contract or a new client account? Is the advice I gave my client correct? Will there be a recession this year? If my company is acquired, will I still have a job? It can also be a lack of certainty in the future of the global economy, politics and business, whether for the short-, medium- or long-term. This impacts the viability of businesses and drives decisions intended to help safeguard their future to the extent possible. Professionals must watch these trends closely to predict what clients are likely to need, and how uncertainty is likely to impact their own clientele.

From Christina's perspective:

"As a partner in a law firm, each year I develop a business plan for my practice and forecast projected billings for my clients. These estimates are based mostly on the pipeline of projects I have for each client and prospective client as well as what the year is projected to look like for their respective businesses. Prognosticating as to whether clients are on an upward trend or likely to have a slower year, and knowing what their

pressure points tend to be, are important factors in bringing more certainty into a situation which can otherwise be tough to predict. On a bigger scale, other partners likewise make these projections for clients, and firms take these estimates into account on an aggregate basis in determining estimated collections for the year. In times where business growth is more uncertain, firms are more conservative in their business expenses and projected budgets which will, in turn, impact targets for hiring, staff salaries, decisions on whether to enter new markets and the like."

From David's perspective:

"My job is all about planning for uncertainty. In law and in business, little is certain; outcomes are rarely known beyond doubt. As in-house counsel, my job is risk management. Risk is born out of uncertainty. My role is to help identify the risks my organization is exposed to and help the business leaders plan accordingly. I start with the legal risks and, working with my business colleagues, help identify the business risks and then together we create plans to manage them. We often have the opportunity to be on the forefront of educating our business colleagues about upcoming uncertainty/risk and help lead the charge to prepare for it."

The Upside of Uncertainty

Uncertainty generally comes with flux and movement, both of which indicate that circumstances are dynamic, and not static. This can bring great opportunity - to grow, stretch, do different things, and to do the same things differently - and better. Sometimes it is hard to see the other side of uncertainty in the moment, but these windows to improve and evolve rarely, if ever, come with just maintaining the status quo.

Uncertainty keeps you on your toes, so that you are better prepared and suffer less disruption in your business, work and life when things go differently than expected. If you have given thought to the possibility of things going sideways, you are prepared, and it is less disruptive and chaotic. We both often say that we have developed a comfort zone of being outside of our comfort zone. David explains, *"I do not know what novel issues will next land on my desk, but I do know that they inevitably will. When they do, I take a deep breath and dive in to figure them out - sometimes it is scary to have so much uncertainty but I have learned to embrace it and use it, to improve and evolve, both for myself and for my company."*

Uncertainty and Resilience Through the COVID-19 Pandemic

The global pandemic and the resulting stay-at-home orders drastically impacted both work and home life for us all. The good news is that many organizations were prepared for this scenario, technologically and otherwise. In many ways, it was business day-to-day, other than the fact that we did not connect with people in person. Video conferencing was a tremendous help in staying connected in a more meaningful way than either on the phone or by email. However, when we stopped working and looked at what was going on around us, there was a profound shift in the world, and this significantly impacted our clients - both as professionals and as people, as well as our businesses. None of us will be the same.

Working at home was the most tangible change for many. The intentionality of our adaptability increased exponentially thereafter. For many who are in positions that require them to be highly collaborative, being in constant communication is imperative to the success of the individual and the team as a whole. One of the toughest difficulties that came with this change was the issue of separating our work and personal lives.

From Christina's perspective:

"Going into the COVID-19 lockdown situation, I had these great visions of having more time to exercise, rest, take care of chores around my house and other tasks. What I found is that I had greater difficulty separating my work from my personal life. I found myself working longer

hours than I had before, not having any downtime and not accomplishing any of the personal goals I had set for myself. It was only once I became more mindful of this issue, that I was able to reaffirm my intent to better create separation so that I could get at least a little bit more rest and clear my head."

From David's perspective:

"As someone who was used to working at home only a few days a year, it was difficult, shifting to working from home full-time. There was no concern with having enough work to do or the motivation to do it; the concern was how to stop working and maintain some semblance of a personal/non-work life. What had been my commute time was added to my work time. I was at my dining room table at 6:00 a.m., working non-stop for the next 12 to 14 hours. I started wearing my regular office attire during the day and changing clothes in the evening as if I were coming home from the office, which helped make a difference in mindset in terms of delineating between work and personal time. I will also say that my dry cleaner was quite happy to see me that first Saturday after I made the change.

My company has multiple business units across the US and in other countries. Even before the pandemic, I was used to working with clients remotely. We have always connected by telephone, email and text, with in-person meetings typically only once or twice a year. When the pandemic started, those communication styles continued with video conferences. The real difference was the quarantine state of mind. In many respects, that isolation can seem greater even if, in fact, we have always worked together remotely from each other. The biggest difference in the way I now stay connected with colleagues and team members is that we check in personally more often, beyond strictly talking business."

The irony about the pandemic lockdown was that while we were all required to exercise social distancing, we as a society were more resourceful in finding ways to both stay close and actually grow closer. We quickly found that little acts of kindness, no matter what they were, would go a long way. This still holds true today, even after life has returned to "normal." Whether it is a quick check-in call, emailing someone to say that you are thinking about them, or having a virtual coffee with a client by video, all of these gestures carry new meaning.

Professionals in a wide range of industries have proven just how resilient and innovative they can be. Networking and relationship building is more important than ever, as individuals seek to reconnect with new and existing clients, colleagues, and referral sources. The good news is we are all in the same boat. The concept of virtual networking is something we are all doing together; it simply has to be accepted as the way to do it. Networking in this new normal is accomplished to a large degree in the same way we have always connected, but we must be intentional about it. Video conferencing is the best way to virtually network, especially with people you are just meeting and getting to know.

With many businesses still choosing to work remotely, even if only part-time, it is important for the lines of communication to remain open for high-performing teams to be successful. Team leads need to regularly assess individual and collective performance across financial and productivity levers, and should have regular meetings to discuss what is working well and where the challenges lie. It is also important for teams to be nimble, resilient and creative in their approach to getting the job done. Patience, understanding and compassion are critical in shifting the mindset from a short-term phenomenon to a longer-term reality.

Although video conferencing is hugely beneficial, there is still something that gets lost by not being together. Many organizations have recognized that this interpersonal glue helps ensure that the workplace culture remains healthy and is a driving force in attracting and retaining talent, thus bringing the majority of their workforce back into the office. There are often efficiencies with resources and technology that may exist in the workplace that do not exist remotely. Being back in the office with your colleagues also makes work more fun and helps alleviate the monotony of being at home.

Deciding how to best strike that balance between in office and from home depends on numerous factors, including who you are, where you work and the level of flexibility in your job. It also matters whether your preference is in alignment with your employer's choices. Christina explains, *"I work at a firm where we have adopted a hybrid approach, and my preference is in alignment with that model. I am an introvert, and while some have called COVID-19 an introvert's dream, I could not work 100% remotely without losing significant elements of my job that I love. The most important is being with people and connecting in person."*

From Christina's perspective:

"When I look back on my career as an associate, there were so many mentoring opportunities I got by virtue of being in my office when a partner happened to walk by with a project they needed help on. There were countless opportunities to develop both professional and personal relationships with my colleagues by virtue of being in the office together, whether by grabbing lunch, coffee or a drink. This would happen spontaneously rather than being scheduled. I do not think I would be where I am today as an attorney and professional if I did not have these opportunities.

Speaking from personal experience, returning to the office was a combination of joy, anticipation, apprehension and sadness for me. Anticipation and joy to see people that I care deeply about and had not seen in a long time. Apprehension because like everyone else, I was concerned about getting COVID-19, and about the possibility of giving it to someone else. Sadness because so much time had passed since we were all last together and things were more normal. Also, because so much had changed for all of us. We all know people who got sick or passed away during the pandemic. Some of them were people with whom we worked closely. The sense that nothing will ever be the same again can be sobering, but is counterbalanced by the happiness of being together again."

From David's perspective:

"For lawyers, especially younger lawyers, associates, and in-house attorneys, it is critical to work in the office a few days a week. For those in their first several years of practice, it is essential to be in the office with more senior attorneys. It is incumbent upon those senior attorneys to help train the next generation. Yes, there is much we can do just as well remotely as in the office. However, there is no substitute for what we can learn simply by being in the same room. Learning how to conduct yourself in different settings requires doing so in person to truly master it. You cannot overstate the value of simply being present to get access to new opportunities. Oftentimes, a senior lawyer or business leader needs help at that moment and will grab someone who is physically near them. You miss those opportunities when you are not in the office, and those ultimately are the drivers of closer relationships and career advancement. Watching other associates in action, and being in meetings and negotiations in person, is how you learn. You get to see how more experienced professionals work. You can see how they conduct themselves in a variety of situations. You cannot get the body language or nuance that underlies the words being spoken through a computer screen. Being live and in person with others is how you best learn to be a professional.

At first, returning to the office after so many months away was quite scary. It was fatiguing and disorienting. However, we moved past that fairly quickly as we got used to going back and being around other people. Yes, many of us developed a fondness for being at home, but do not underestimate the negative impacts of loneliness that you may not be aware of when you are only at home. Also, remember to consciously practice patience and kindness with everyone, not only your colleagues, but also people outside of work who may have had a rough time. A little kindness goes a long way."

While the pandemic left an indelible mark on each aspect of our lives, there has been some good that has emerged. Making it through the pandemic has been empowering and put circumstances that pre-pandemic we viewed as tough into a whole different perspective. It is inevitable that our frames of reference have changed compared to what our day-to-day existence was before and during the pandemic, and we have become more resilient in the process. The struggles we have been forced to overcome - and the losses so many of us have experienced - have taught us the importance of gratitude for each day we are given to make a difference in this world.

Recommendations For When You are Faced with Uncertainty

When your circumstances are causing you to feel uncertain as to how best to move forward, shift your perspective, reframe your approach and plan accordingly. Remember that it is a marathon, not a sprint; be innovative and try several approaches to see which are the most successful and adjust. Regularly assess what is most effective and most challenging for you, what leads to the most successful results and address whatever issues there are in real time. To the extent you need assistance from others to handle these challenges, do not be shy about seeking help.

Remember we are all learning as we go. We all have challenging circumstances to navigate, so be patient with others and be understanding. Be open to change in ways you may not have been previously, and embrace the inevitable as opportunities to reinvent yourself and your approach. Now is a great time to try out something new.

Innovation, Technology and Artificial Intelligence: Growth in Motion

Innovation and technology are not just buzzwords. They are the beating heart of progress, the quiet (sometimes loud) revolution that transforms how we work, think, lead, connect and live. Whether we embrace or resist them, innovation and technology are always moving. The question becomes: Are we evolving with them?

Depending on the individual or organization, innovation can take many shapes. For some, it might mean offering services in a better, more efficient or more value-driven way. For others, it is about increasing the quality and quantity of products while minimizing effort, waste and cost. Sometimes, it is about solving one problem while simultaneously considering the ripple effects across the business and the community. Other times, innovation is doing what has never been done before, whether that is something others have imagined but could not implement, or something no one has even dared to dream of.

At its core, innovation is progress. It is also momentum and creativity in action. The word itself means introducing something new - an idea, a method, a mindset. Innovation pushes us beyond what is comfortable and challenges us to evolve, both individually and collectively. In many cases, it asks us to partner across traditional silos. Departments, disciplines and industries must collaborate to co-create better outcomes. In today's world, staying in your own lane is not enough. To remain relevant, effective and meaningful, we must think wider, reach further and build smarter.

The Case for Constant Evolution

Being innovative does not mean being flashy. It means being aware and vigilant. It represents growth, maturity, progress and relevance, especially in a 24/7 world that is moving and shifting incessantly. The ability to innovate separates the good from the exceptional, the stagnant from the thriving.

As professionals, leaders and people, we face increasingly complex problems. We cannot afford to keep using the same playbook for every new challenge. Our ability to adapt and approach problems from fresh, creative angles is not just helpful; it is *necessary*. It gives us an edge in business development, client service, and how we live and lead.

There is a Steve Jobs quote that still captures the soul of innovation many years later. When asked if he conducted market research for a project, Jobs responded that he didn't, because customers *"don't know what they want until you show it to them."* That is innovation at its most powerful - leading people to discover needs they do not yet realize they have.

When we innovate, we lead, shape, anticipate and problem solve. We are serving a higher purpose. And when we do it well, our clients, colleagues and communities come to see us not just as providers but as valued partners and visionaries.

Innovation is a Culture, Not Just a Concept

Implementing new ideas can be very challenging. It cannot be done in isolation, and it rarely works if we try to bulldoze our way through resistance. Culture eats strategy for breakfast, and innovation, by definition, threatens the status quo.

To innovate effectively, we need to understand the culture within which we are working. What does our organization value? How do our senior leaders make decisions? Who needs to be in the room, and who needs to hear the idea first to champion it? Moving individuals is one thing. Moving an organization takes strategy, patience and influence. It starts by building a coalition of leaders who believe in the vision and are willing to help support it - then change becomes possible. And often, one innovation begets another. Innovation is contagious, but so is fear. So, our focus needs to be on speaking to people in ways they can hear us (use your EQ), to meet them where they are and then, step by step, to move forward together.

Technology: A Double-Edged Tool

There is no question that technology has made our lives easier as professionals. Over the past few decades, it has transformed how we access clients, gather information and deliver services. Virtual private networks (VPNs), cloud-based desktops and video conferencing tools have allowed us to create functional offices from anywhere in the world. Smartphones put people and answers at our fingertips, and remote collaboration tools allow us to be global without ever leaving our homes. Email, social media and cloud-based systems have revolutionized how we communicate and store data. We are faster, more efficient and more connected than ever. And, with artificial intelligence (AI) evolving at breakneck speed, the speed of transformation is accelerating by the second.

Technology has also leveled our playing field. Sole practitioners and small businesses can now compete with corporate giants in ways which had previously been impossible. A stable Internet connection, a well-designed website, and a strong digital presence can open doors that never used to exist.

However, technology has also raised expectations, and not always in healthy ways. In the past, we had buffers built into communication. There was time to think, reflect and compose. Today, our inboxes are always bursting, our phones are always on, and people expect real-time responses. What once took days now takes minutes or less. And our stress levels skyrocket when the Internet goes out or a server crashes. For many professionals, the pace of technology has eroded the space we need for critical thinking, analysis and rest, and comes at a huge cost.

Contrary to popular belief, professional value is tied not to how fast we can respond but to *how well we think*. Technology should be a tool for innovation, not a treadmill we cannot get off of. If we are not careful, the very tools designed to empower us will start to control us. So we have to set boundaries, preserve time to be thoughtful and strategic, and protect our creativity for the asset it is.

Artificial Intelligence

Artificial intelligence, as a concept and tool, incorporates so many different things. The term has been part of our vernacular for quite a while, and it has quickly evolved from being this vague concept referring to the notion of computers doing tasks that have historically been done by people, to being everywhere all the time in every facet of our lives. There is very little in our society these days that is not touched by AI somehow, much like the Internet 25 years ago. It is transforming the world as we know it, and as with many things that we have seen during the course of history, it is incredibly powerful, and it is up to us to leverage its capabilities for the betterment of our lives, and to put sufficient guardrails in place to mitigate against its malevolent use.

David explains, *"As a lifelong Star Trek fan and having watched the first Terminator movie the night after my Contracts final first semester of law school, the fact that we seem to be on the precipice of the actual AI age is exciting and concerning at the same time."* What we will ultimately be able to use AI for both in life and in the practice of law, and how things will actually change over time, triggers some concern about the negative implications, especially for younger people just entering the practice of law, and for the job market generally.

From Christina's perspective:

"My use of AI in my practice, much like the technology itself, is evolving. Given where I am in my career, both being in private practice as

well as practicing for over 30 years, my use of AI looks very different day-to-day than for more junior lawyers. I have seen so much in my career, and rarely am I starting from scratch with my knowledge of an area or for developing frameworks within which to address those issues. I find AI tools particularly helpful when I am trying to update my understanding of a current issue and need some direction on where to turn to get that information quickly. My firm, like many others, has a set of law-related AI applications that are part of the suite of tools available to our workforce (and clients as appropriate), some of which you may not even think have AI running in the background."

From David's perspective:

"I have only recently begun actively experimenting with various AI platforms in my practice. I anticipate that I will increasingly and intentionally use AI tools in much the same way Tina described, particularly AI tools built specifically for lawyers, not simply the AI built into existing platforms like Microsoft Outlook to suggest email sentence completion or AI-generated internet search results for information about a TV show. Thus far, I have experimented using AI to help with initial drafts of some non-standard contract clauses, which has been surprisingly helpful, and to generate presentation outlines, with mixed results so far, though I have been pleasantly surprised to see similarities with outlines I wrote on my own the old-fashioned way using my own brain power. As AI tools become more robust and reliable, I envision using them to help with initial research into new or unfamiliar substantive areas of law and to help get past writer's block."

It is incumbent upon us to ensure that our use of AI aligns with various considerations, including compliance with our organization's AI policy and the policies of our clients. There are also important attorney-client privilege and confidentiality concerns, as well as weaknesses and gaps with the technology as it stands today, such as hallucinations. Lawyers also have a code of ethics to which we need to adhere, so ensuring the completeness and accuracy of the work product we generate while leveraging AI is of paramount importance. AI should always be used with good common sense as the backdrop, as with everything else, and used in moderation and with intentionality, particularly given where we are in its evolution.

A primary concern among many professionals is that using AI will cause a degradation and outright loss of people's ability to engage in critical thinking, analysis and writing. Another pitfall, given the promise of doing things faster, is that the demands on us to produce even more work and more quickly will steadily increase, which in turn will lead to a tremendous increase in the stress and burden of practicing law, along with an ever-diminishing ability to take a break. The idea might be that we work fewer hours because we can get things done faster, but the concern is that the opposite will in fact be true. Finally, there is the threat that some lawyers will neglect to read what AI produces for them and fail to recognize that what they are writing and citing in their briefs are in fact erroneous AI hallucinations.

Innovation Beyond Invention

Too often, when discussing innovation we focus solely on invention, such as the breakthroughs in science, medicine and technology that grab headlines and change history. But this unfairly narrow lens leaves many who are worthy among us out of the conversation. Innovation does not always come with a patent, nor does it have to be revolutionary to be powerful. Innovation can show up in how we solve problems, build relationships, approach leadership, and even in how we prioritize wellness in the workplace.

Innovation can be simple, subtle and quiet. It can be reimagining a client intake process, rethinking how we support team development, or finding more inclusive communication methods. The key is always the same: *Does this create progress?* That is where we start.

The Myth of the Lightning Bolt

In his book *Where Good Ideas Come From: The Natural History of Innovation*, Steven Johnson debunks the myth that innovation results from a sudden flash of brilliance. He reminds us that most breakthroughs are slow burns, ideas that evolve over time, built through collaboration, iteration and yes, failure.

Real innovation often comes not from the lab but from the lunchroom, not from the grind but from the gap, from taking a walk, reading something unexpected or letting your mind wander as you go about your day. The best ideas do not always come when we are *trying* to be brilliant. They often come when we create the space to connect the dots already floating around in our minds. We have to be willing to pause, play, daydream, experiment, ask questions and occasionally get it wrong. This requires humility, curiosity and trust - not just in ourselves, but in each other.

Collaboration is a Catalyst

If there is one truth about innovation, it is that it rarely happens in isolation. Even the most brilliant minds need connection. We need each other to challenge assumptions, offer perspectives and co-create solutions that are bigger and better than what any one of us could do alone. Too often though, we resist collaboration out of fear - fear of being wrong, looking foolish or losing control. But perfection is not the goal - growth and progress are. We should stop trying to be right all the time and start stepping out of our comfort zone because the magic happens in conversation and connection.

When we leverage our collective experiences, talents and ideas, we create something far more innovative than any individual could dream up alone.

Create the Conditions for Innovation

Innovation is not something you wait for - it is something you *invite*. And that invitation begins by making space for it. Just like technology companies build in time for creativity, such as Google's famous 20% rule, we too need to give ourselves permission to step away from the grind and into imagination. We must unplug, reflect and reconnect with our values and goals. We need to ask: *What are we doing? Why are we doing it? And is there a better way?*

When we slow down, we begin to notice what is possible. And often, the most meaningful innovation is not about doing something new. It is about seeing what was there all along in a new light. Ultimately, innovation is a mindset. Whether we are leveraging technology to better serve our clients, creating new systems that make our organizations more efficient, or simply finding a new way to approach an old problem, innovation is always about one thing: *growth*.

Innovation asks us to stretch, risk and reimagine. It invites us to lead with curiosity instead of certainty, collaborate instead of compete, and evolve instead of entrench. In doing so, it helps us become not only better professionals but better humans.

Pro Bono, Volunteering and Extracurriculars

Now more than ever, there is a collective realization that giving back is not just "the right thing to do"—it is also a powerful tool for personal, professional and community transformation. These efforts stretch beyond charity—they are acts of leadership, humanity and legacy. There are more individuals and organizations than ever before with legal needs for which they are unable to pay. Sometimes it is truly a matter of life or death. There is also increased awareness that these needs are both local and global, and there are many ways for US-based lawyers to meaningfully assist people abroad. This has led to more flexibility with pro bono and a real willingness to engage in creative and collaborative partnerships with clients, potential clients, trade associations, governments and various other organizations, both within and outside the US, and this has opened the doors to pro bono opportunities and volunteering that did not exist before.

Pro bono work has always been an important part of the profession and the professional requirements for practicing lawyers. Over the years, there have been some very creative initiatives and a greater push to get more attorneys involved in pro bono work, both in law firms and in the in-house world. Law firms and in-house departments have been launching various cooperative partnerships in which both in-house and private practice lawyers work together to provide pro bono services. This includes staffing legal aid clinics and forming creative partnerships with nonlegal organizations, such as legal-medical partnerships in which lawyers and hospitals team up to provide pro bono help to families and individuals trying to navigate issues such as Medicaid and its maze of paperwork.

Remember that civic service is about service to others, not to promote yourself. Pro bono work, volunteering and board service are a means of giving back to your community, not to pad your resume.

Finding Quality Pro Bono Opportunities

There are endless opportunities for everyone to make a meaningful difference with pro bono, regardless of their practice area and years of experience. So many firms, corporations, bar associations, nonprofit organizations and other entities have or are in the process of institutionalizing pro bono programs with a myriad of litigation and transactional opportunities. Unfortunately, there is never a shortage of these needs, and it is just a matter of going out and finding them if they do not typically cross your path.

Law firm lawyers generally have greater access to a broader selection of pro bono opportunities than in-house lawyers. This is in large part due to the fact that many law firms, large ones in particular, have developed their own pro bono platforms, with an infrastructure built around providing their attorneys with a wide variety of choices. These days, many firms are opening these opportunities to clients and in-house counsel, not just their firm's lawyers. Trade associations such as the Association of Corporate Counsel partner with various law firms to provide their membership with access to a wide array of pro bono matters that up until recently were not easily accessible to in-house counsel.

For in-house lawyers, one challenge when looking for quality pro bono work is finding work within their specialty. We encourage lawyers to use pro bono work as a way to spread their wings beyond their comfort zone. They can look at pro bono work not just as a way to help others in need, but also as a way to learn something new and expand their skills in the process.

Breaking into the Non-Profit Board Arena

Board service is another way to give back. There are myriad ways to get onto boards. First, you need to think about where your interests and passions lie with respect to civic service. There are so many organizations to choose from, each with different missions, causes and ways in which they operate. Likewise, boards can significantly vary in terms of their level of activity, what they are seeking to accomplish and what they expect and demand of board members. You need to do your homework and understand what serving on a particular board entails.

You also need to understand that getting onto boards is often a process and may take time. You should figure out the best way to meet the people you need to be successful in your efforts. Sometimes, you must first be a volunteer at the organization, or you may need to reach out to existing board members and the executive director to learn more about how best to become involved. There may be people in your network who are past or present board members who can lend a hand. Other times, you may first need to develop a high enough profile within your community so that you are chosen to serve on the board, rather than the other way around. There are many possibilities, and the right one depends on you, your personality and the board on which you are interested in serving.

The board process may not be easy, especially when just starting out. Consider where your passions and commitments lie. If you are unsure, try volunteering with different organizations to learn what they are about, and which fit best with your interests. If your sights are set on a high-profile board when you are just starting out in your volunteer career, you may first need to get your feet wet with a smaller organization. Learn what it means to serve on a non-profit board and how board work fits within your life. Develop your reputation as a reliable and desirable board member. By demonstrating your interest and willingness to help others and being actively involved, in due time, you can move up to that high-profile board.

Finding The Right Balance

You need to be honest and realistic about your level of interest and commitment, both to yourself and to those recruiting you to join their board. You need to be very clear on where all of your priorities lie and where civic service fits into the grand scheme. This will drive your assessment as to how much time and energy you have and are willing to give to civic service. You also need to have a thorough understanding of a given non-profit's expectations and demands on your time and where it fits in with respect to everything else in your life. Knowing all of these things will help you to strike that delicate balance.

If joining a board is too big of a time commitment for you, volunteer for a committee, help organize a discrete program, or even do just one task for the organization. This way, you fulfill a genuine need, you feel a greater sense of connection to the organization and put in just the right amount of time.

Changing The Way People View Lawyers

It is unfortunate that people's perceptions of lawyers are sometimes quite negative, based on the few bad apples out there. Even though every profession has them, the public is often less forgiving of lawyers, possibly because of the special ethical duties and responsibilities lawyers have, and the gravity of the issues that attorneys typically handle. Christina explains, *"My first real exposure to these negative sentiments was when I was in engineering school. Many of my instructors and classmates believed that lawyers readily put a price on someone's life and that they show no remorse in doing so, particularly in the product liability context."*

What critics don't seem to appreciate is that lawyers are human beings just like everyone else, and that they care just as much, if not more so, about others than anyone else. People are often reminded of this when they see lawyers out in the community lending a hand on a pro bono basis to those who are less fortunate. Hopefully, as an increasing number of lawyers become involved in civic service, these unfair notions will be dispelled. When laypersons see lawyers giving their time, it enables them to see lawyers in another light - as fellow members of the community, lending their time and expertise to help others, at no charge.

Meeting Annual Pro Bono Goals

There can be a number of challenges when it comes to meeting annual pro bono goals, including finding the right subject matter for you. Some attorneys like to stick with their practice area, while others view pro bono as an opportunity to venture into a completely different specialty. The challenge then becomes finding someone to provide you with the necessary assistance to ensure that the matter is being handled properly. It can also be a struggle to find enough time to take on a pro bono matter. Depending on how active your matter becomes, it can be tough to balance the demands of pro bono with the needs of your everyday practice. From an organizational perspective, it is sometimes difficult to make sure that all lawyers are prioritizing pro bono and doing their part to ensure that the organization's overall pro bono goals are being met.

For in-house attorneys, one of the greatest challenges is finding pro bono opportunities that include malpractice insurance. Most in-house attorneys do not carry malpractice insurance, thus limiting their ability to handle matters for clients other than their employer. Another challenge may be licensing. In-house attorneys working under multi-jurisdictional practice rules in states other than their home state are typically limited by such rules to representing only their employer. Fortunately, that practice is changing, and some states, including Illinois, now allow licensed attorneys to also handle pro bono matters *(check applicable rules for details)*.

The Importance of Activities Outside of Work

It is important to have interests beyond your job responsibilities for a number of reasons. First, if these activities are chosen mindfully, they can enable you to have professional experiences that you may not otherwise get. Whether they are hobbies such as coin collecting, painting, mentoring or volunteering for a nonprofit, extracurricular activities provide many important benefits. You can develop certain skills, be exposed to new types of situations and gain knowledge that you otherwise would not acquire in your everyday job. Extracurricular activities are an opportunity to do something beneficial for and with others, and can provide the opportunity to meet new people, and to learn different perspectives and even new approaches to problem solving. You can also take what you learn and bring it to work to make your job performance even better.

It is important that you participate in activities that are meaningful to you, where you think you can contribute and where you believe you will be better for having the experience. Also, be sure that you meet as many people as possible so that you can make the most of the networking aspect of your activities. In addition, be sure to connect the dots before you say yes; think through whether the opportunity is likely to help you to accomplish your professional goals and to leverage your skills, contacts and interests such that one plus one equals three. And be sure to revisit all of these activities periodically to confirm that your participation still makes sense, and to step out of them if they no longer serve their purpose.

Be sure to ask enough questions to evaluate whether they are the right activities for you right now. Be clear on what you are trying to accomplish. Is this for professional growth and advancement? Or is it just for fun? You also should get clarity about what the time commitment is and whether there are requirements like hosting meetings or events, which may tip the balance. Finally, make sure that you are going to enjoy yourself. Anytime that you commit to something beyond your job, it is important to ensure that you find it worthwhile enough to outweigh the price of participation, both in dollars and in time spent away from your family, and any other trade-offs you may be making.

David explains, *"I remain passionate about the causes and the organizations I serve, however, 15 years is a long time on one board. It is important to recognize that burnout can start to set in, and also that there comes a time to make room for others with new ideas. It is also important to recognize when you just need a break from doing organized extracurricular activities. After 30 years serving on boards, I needed a break so I took two years off. Once I had the opportunity to step back, I was then ready to join another nonprofit board. The break let me recharge. It also allowed me to consider what I can bring to a new board by building on my past experience."*

Insights Into Our Unique Pro Bono Experiences

From Christina's perspective:

"I began my career at my first firm as a real estate lawyer with a focus on environmental law. Within a couple of months of joining the firm, a special project came in from Chicago City Hall. I was asked if I would be willing to join the City of Chicago Department of Buildings for several months to help it restructure the Chicago Building Code. The department was in the process of reviewing and revising the building code from cover to cover and wanted to include an outside lawyer as part of the process. My engineering background was a real asset for this project since there are many technical references within the code. The project went on for about half a year and I learned a great deal. It also helped me to understand how important relationships are, both personally and professionally. It was an amazing experience and I had a chance to meet Mayor Daley at the end of the project.

Now, when it comes to selecting pro bono work, I look at a few things, including the practice areas involved, how much time the matter is likely to take and the time frame within which it needs to be completed. I compare this against how much time I have and the type of project in which I am interested at that juncture. If I am likely to need the assistance of others, either within or outside of my practice area, I also consider the availability of those who am I am likely to tap before taking on the case.

The senior leadership at both of the law firms at which I have practiced have delivered the clear message that serving the underprivileged is the right thing to do and is essential. My first firm's leadership were key architects in creating its innovative international pro bono platform. Pro bono is required of every attorney at many large firms, including my current firm. We also actively partner with numerous clients on different pro bono activities, and it is an integral part of our business development efforts."

From David's perspective:

"Shortly after I started practicing law, I joined the board of a homeless shelter and services provider in Uptown Chicago. In addition to my board service, I provided legal advice to the organization over the years, including such things as responding to records subpoenas, various employment issues and drafting personnel policies and procedures. The bulk of my pro bono activities since going in-house have been participating in activities for improving the practice of law and the legal profession through volunteer service with the Association of Corporate Counsel. This includes not only through serving on the board of directors but also helping plan and present continuing education programs, helping run a summer internship program for law students and helping the ACC Chicago Chapter expand pro bono opportunities.

I am fortunate to work for a company which is owned by committed philanthropists. Our culture embraces the necessity and importance of giving back. I am also fortunate to have a boss who has supported all of my volunteer efforts over the years."

We all must remember those who are not as fortunate as we are and consider how we can help them. We must do our part to make a positive difference for those who are unable to fend for themselves. Consider whether there are pro bono cases you may want to take on that could help an individual or group in need of some type of assistance. Perhaps there are young students, or even rookie attorneys, who would benefit from meeting with you to discuss their potential career paths. Maybe there is a charity or organization that could greatly benefit from your time or money. Take time to visit a sick or elderly friend or family member, or to wrap and deliver presents for children whose families cannot afford to buy them. The possibilities are endless. Whatever you choose, however you decide to give back, know that your efforts and dedication matter.

We often believe that others are doing just as well, if not better, than we are. We tend to minimize the importance of the contributions we can make to others and to society. As lawyers, we are in a unique position to help people in ways that others simply cannot. Whether we are helping the wrongfully convicted, mentoring future lawyers, or providing financial assistance to the needy, know that anything we do for another person, either big or small, can have a profound impact and can change the course of lives. What better gift is there - to give or receive?

Skills of a Great Professional

This chapter is devoted to just some of the countless skills of a great lawyer. While this is by no means a comprehensive list, we explore some of what, in our experience, are the most important attributes of the exceptional lawyers and mentors with whom we have had the pleasure of working and learning from.

Being Indispensable

Being indispensable means that you are essential and mission-critical. You are crucial to have as part of the team and the organization. You are necessary to accomplish a particular goal, in making it through the day to day, and an invaluable part of the decision-making team such that your input is not only desired but essential before a final decision is made.

In the context of practicing law, this term is often used to refer to a particular skillset or combination of qualities that you bring to the table that makes you someone people feel they cannot live without. This is essentially a client-focused concept. For in-house attorneys, the goal is to become indispensable to both the business as well as other attorneys in the legal department. The same concept holds true within law firms, as you not only want to be indispensable to your clients but also to other lawyers at your firm.

As with many aspects of our legal careers, becoming indispensable starts with getting to know as much as possible about your client's business; this goes for both in-house and outside counsel. In addition to gaining a deep understanding of what your client's business is and how it works, you should also get to know the businesspeople - the C-suite and beyond; learn what they do, what is important to them, and how they do their jobs. Get to know them as people; learn to speak their language. The easiest way to accomplish this is to ask them questions and carefully listen to their answers. Demonstrate by your conduct that you are a dependable and essential part of the team, as invested in the outcome as they are.

If you are indispensable to your clients, you are better able to provide meaningful advice, help your client manage risk and avoid unnecessary and costly missteps. You are also more likely to be valued and retained. Being indispensable also enhances career enjoyment and fulfillment.

As organizations evolve over time, so do the workforces within them. Employees have different experiences over the years which drive their capabilities, relationships, responsibilities and tenure. These factors all impact performance of the individuals and the teams they comprise. Hopefully, people are given the opportunity to fulfill a role that is not duplicated by anyone else on the team and for which they are uniquely qualified and needed. As one matures in their career, they can then become indispensable in any number of different ways, which helps ensure that they continue a long and meaningful professional trajectory over time.

What makes you indispensable today does not necessarily make you so tomorrow. We have seen instances where people spend a lot of effort trying to convince others that they are indispensable without doing the hard work of actually becoming so - and then a situation arises where it becomes evident that life can and will go on without that person. We have also seen the flip side - where people are not given the credit that they deserve until they leave an organization, and then it becomes clear that they have been undervalued. The moral of the story is to remain keenly aware of what you and those around you bring to the table, both individually as well as collectively, and manage and lead your team from that place.

Another step to becoming indispensable - bring solutions, not just problems, and train your clients and business colleagues that they need to immediately call you, even if they are not sure whether it is a legal question. Then make yourself available, listen to them and provide a solution. By demonstrating your versatility in your willingness to work on a broad variety of matters, and being practical with your advice to better minimize risk and maximize the chances of a successful outcome, you can show your colleagues, clients and management that you are an indispensable member of the team.

Being Nimble

As we balance our goals, work and family routines, we should be mindful that change remains the constant undercurrent in our lives. Nothing is static and we are constantly on the move, which presents myriad opportunities and challenges. While all of this uncertainty can make us uncomfortable and apprehensive, it is in our best interest to both adapt and leverage this dynamic reality to our advantage. Being nimble is a critical part of this equation.

Merriam-Webster's Dictionary defines "nimble" as, *"quick and light in motion,"* and *"marked by quick, alert, clever conception, comprehension, or resourcefulness."* While these two concepts are interrelated, they are actually quite different and call upon distinct skillsets. One relates to action and movement and feels reactive, while the other describes one's thought process, is strategic and seems more proactive. Both concepts provide us with useful guidance for navigating the ups and downs of today's business environment and help ensure that we are responding appropriately.

Being nimble enables us to adapt and react to the rapidly changing circumstances which impact our clients' businesses on a daily basis. We are able to see how their needs may be evolving and respond to events in their environment, and consider how we may need to quickly alter our tack in order to effectively address the circumstances they are currently facing. As nimble practitioners, we are not discouraged by the possibility that our past recipes for success no longer work and that we may need to self-correct. Instead, we are flexible, resilient and able to respond quickly to the current reality. We seek to understand the genesis of change and where it is likely to lead in an effort to enhance predictability and so that we can better position our clients and ourselves for what is next.

There are many ways in which our practices can benefit when we are nimble. We are better able to create business opportunities in the face of uncertainty. We can quickly and accurately predict changes that may be afoot which are likely to impact our clients' organizations, and we are able to adjust our approach accordingly. Sometimes these changes are swift and can range anywhere from significant events in the life cycle of their businesses such as acquisitions, divestitures or compliance issues to a forced change of counsel due to an unexpected conflict. Whatever the situation, being nimble enables us to be there for our clients in their hour of need in a more meaningful way and to continuously demonstrate our value as their trusted advisor. We are not intimidated by the prospect of expanding our existing client relationships beyond just our area of expertise. Rather, we embrace the opportunity to learn more about all of their legal business needs and to take a more holistic approach in our work with them.

These types of efforts are both welcomed by clients and can pay great dividends in the long run. Being nimble also enables us to be more strategic in the ways in which we develop relationships with prospective clients. This is particularly true during challenging times such as a recession, when there is significant disruption in the market and when the old rules no longer apply. At such times, it often becomes more difficult to find ways to differentiate ourselves. We must all demonstrate both sophisticated substantive talents and equally important soft skills, which are often tied to high performance and critical areas such as client service and relationship management.

Being nimble is another arrow in our emotional intelligence quiver and enables us to effectively strike this delicate balance from one potential client to the next. No two businesses have the same legal needs and by being nimble, we are able to quickly discern how best to present our capabilities in a way that resonates with our audience and to adapt to swiftly changing circumstances during our initial meetings and communications. We are able to think outside the box, spot issues and provide logic and insight as to how best to address them. Being thoughtfully and strategically quick on our feet provides another way we can meaningfully stand apart from our competition.

Just as our clients are barraged with new opportunities and challenges on a daily basis, so are we. It is very important for us to nimbly position our organizations and ourselves with the same amount of savvy and foresight as we bring to our clients. This means that we must be vigilant about the business of our business and must never lose sight of those qualities which will ensure our short and long-term success. We need to regularly evaluate what effectively distinguishes us in a particular geographic market, within certain practice areas and in a given business sector. We should be continuously aware of who our competition currently is and who it is likely to be tomorrow as well as those characteristics which successfully differentiate us all from one another. By doing so, we can more accurately predict how certain issues are likely to evolve over time and more effectively leverage these changes into opportunities for our organizations and ourselves.

Being Multidimensional

Being multidimensional means that you bring qualities, talents and attributes to the fore, which enable you to tackle numerous issues and myriad matters with aplomb. You are able to analyze situations from different points of view which are appropriate for the circumstances. You are able to communicate, strategize and execute wearing a variety of hats. You are resilient, flexible and nimble. It includes drawing upon a combination of legal knowledge, business knowledge, emotional intelligence, and an understanding and awareness of other areas such as culture and current events. The ability to do this is facilitated by having multiple and varied interests in life. You might look at it as the diversity within you.

This is invaluable from both client service and leadership perspectives. It enables you to be more out of the box and non-linear in your thought process and gives you the ability to be more effective in your problem solving. It provides different lenses through which to observe the world and the ability to empathize with clients and colleagues so that you can avoid having tunnel vision. Being multidimensional enables you to work with many different types of clients with ease and to work with the same client across many different situations. It is not so much about being the subject matter expert across distinct legal areas as it is having a heightened awareness and sensitivity that enables you to meaningfully contribute in various situations to address the relevant issues quickly and effectively, either on your own or with the assistance of others you choose to bring in. We live in a world where lawyers need to differentiate themselves, and this is one way to do just that.

The broader your interests and curiosity, and the more you are open to new experiences, the better equipped you will be to approach client matters from different angles and to advise your client not just on black letter law but within a context that makes a practical difference for their needs. Being multidimensional makes it easier to form relationships with different types of people, which not only leads to being a better and more successful lawyer, but also leads to more fulfillment in life generally. For example, most attorneys will agree that the excitement of contract drafting tends to wane after drafting hundreds of them. Boredom can lead to mistakes. So, it is important to find ways to maintain your interest and thereby sharpen your focus on what is truly important in the contract. This is considered taking "the 50,000-foot view" of a situation to understand what the contract means in the larger context of a company's business, the customer's business, even the economy as a whole. This will help you to better understand the broader benefits and pitfalls beyond the document in front of you, which leads to better lawyering and greater career satisfaction.

It is a delicate balance between being multidimensional, and a specialist who requires frequent evaluation and recalibration. The right balance is highly dependent on where you are now and what you want to achieve in your career. If your goal is to have a thriving prolific practice, you must be a great lawyer, stay on top of new developments, continuously look for ways to perfect your craft, make yourself known and to differentiate yourself in the market. If your objective is to be in leadership, there are skills you need to develop and hone that go far beyond just being a respected practitioner and typically involve a level of executive coaching and management training that will help you develop your skills. Striking the right balance requires you to be strategic and to prioritize what is of greatest importance to you. It is a highly personalized exercise.

Finding a balance between being multidimensional and a generalist involves handling many different substantive legal matters that arise across multiple business sectors, involving myriad factual scenarios. Being multidimensional helps you to understand and give advice that better meets the overall goals and needs of your clients. It also helps you to work well with many different people at all levels within your organization and with your customers and vendors. David explains, *"I think it is also why I thrive on the variety and breadth of my practice and the rapidity with which new matters come to me every day, enabling me to constantly be learning and growing as an attorney and as a person."*

Being Unique

When you are unique, you stand apart from the rest. You have a skillset, attitude and approach that make you different. When people look at the totality of who you are - your personality, your talents, your clients, your actions and your contributions to the profession - they automatically know it is you, even if your name is not mentioned. There is a lot of self-awareness that comes with the territory, as well as the ability to authentically embrace who you are as both a professional and an individual. You need to be able to own what makes you unique and you should not be afraid to follow the beat of your own drum.

There are certain guitar players who you know just by hearing them play a song, such as Eric Clapton or Jerry Garcia, or just by hearing their voices, such as Bruce Springsteen or Bob Dylan. Being a unique lawyer is similar in many ways. They are known for certain specialties or skills that instantly set them apart. Some lawyers are unique because they have a practice that few others share, or they have developed a reputation for being distinguished among other practitioners in their specialty. Some lawyers are notable for doing things in a particular, ideally positive, way. Maybe you are known for your cross examination or conflict resolution skills. Uniqueness may lie in superior writing talent or advocacy skills. You may have a knack for relationship building or management skills. These are the things that differentiate, that set you apart when others think about you, or that make others think of you when they are in need of a particular skillset.

Oftentimes it is a delicate balance of knowing when to stand out and when to blend into the group. You want to stand out for positive, selfless reasons, such as doing a great job on a client project or in a pro bono case. It should not be premeditated on your part, and you should not be standing out for the sake of standing out. When tooting your own horn is appropriate, it should be done thoughtfully, carefully and respectfully. For example, when doing business development, you should focus on those skills that make you valuable and unique and play up your strengths. This will help potential clients to distinguish you from your competition much more easily. You should always be respectful and avoid gratuitously criticizing your competition, since that is unseemly and unprofessional.

Sometimes it is better to blend in when, for example, you are working on getting a project done and out the door. That is when being collaborative and a team player are most important. Everyone on the team has an invaluable contribution to make. While there are certain team members who will inevitably stand out more than others, such as the team leader, they should not be forceful or overly assertive about it. It is important that everyone works well together and is collaborative rather than engaging in power struggles.

Blend in by showing that you fit with the organization's culture, mission and platform, but again, only so far as to ensure you do not stick out like a sore thumb and make others turn the other way. You want to blend in to the point that others consider you a team player. At the same time, you want to make sure you maintain your individuality and demonstrate that you are an impact player and making a positive difference.

Young lawyers need to focus on standing out for the right reasons. These include doing great work, working incredibly hard and showing maturity and wisdom. There is simply no substitute for having that fire in the belly and a willingness to go through brick walls for clients. They should demonstrate that they are deep thinkers, highly intellectual and emotionally intelligent, and that they have a strong business savvy.

Young lawyers also need to demonstrate drive, focus and integrity. Show that you are not afraid of the difficult work or long hours. Demonstrate perseverance, poise and determination when working on difficult assignments under demanding circumstances. It is also important not to complain about the long hours and hard work. That will get you noticed, but not in a positive way. Be a leader and speak up with solutions when there are problems.

Being Creative

Another way to stand out is to be creative, someone who can think outside the box and who is able to see issues from a variety of angles and perspectives. Creativity is realizing that the best solutions for clients are often a hybrid of good lawyering, good business and good common sense. Creative lawyers ask clients what the ultimate objective is in a given situation and ask them what they are trying to achieve. They realize that there are often a myriad of ways clients can achieve their goal, and those options usually pose different levels of legal and business risks, costs and short and long-term impacts to the business. Sometimes the optimal solution entails a minimal amount of substantive lawyering but nevertheless presents a great opportunity for creative lawyers to put on their business hat and to serve as a trusted business advisor. A creative lawyer is also someone who can effectively put themselves in the shoes of their clients and other interested parties and understand where they are coming from and how their viewpoints factor into reaching the best solutions. They can meaningfully brainstorm without constraint and, once all the ideas are out on the table, they can then go back and figure out which solutions are optimal.

Creativity encompasses more than just good writing and coming up with novel solutions, although they are important components of being creative. It also means discerning ways to effectively communicate with clients, opponents and colleagues. This can be done in different ways, such as by conducting training sessions on various topics and discussing why they are important to the business and the consequences of various choices. Other aspects of creative lawyering include a willingness to try new things and challenging assumptions - just because it has never been done before does not mean it is wrong. Also, collaborate and seek input from colleagues - teamwork can lead to very creative solutions.

When it comes to a lawyer's individual style, there are a number of key factors. The most obvious is our outward appearance, including how we dress and present ourselves. Our demeanor is another critical component, and it transcends how we look and drives how we come across to others. Our demeanor refers to those qualities and characteristics which others notice about us and what they would say when describing us. It is a critically important aspect of our style, and there should be alignment between how we think we come across and how others actually view us. Disconnects in this regard can often be tricky to navigate and can have significant consequences. Indeed, our demeanor is inextricably linked to our overall effectiveness with other aspects of our style, including how we perform and in our approach to clients and business development efforts. Our style often makes the difference in our ability to land that new client or to resolve a difficult case.

We can all learn a lot from watching others and seeing what works and what does not. But we must then take stock of those qualities and characteristics which resonate the most, tweak them and carry them forward. Developing a unique and creative style that works should give us a level of comfort, confidence and self-assurance which then optimizes our interactions with others and enables them to feel like they know us and what we are all about. Predictability is key, and is all about balance and nuance.

We need to be authentic but also act within acceptable bounds based on our environments and audiences. While we all want to meaningfully distinguish ourselves from the crowd, we want to stand out for the right reasons rather than the wrong ones.

Navigating Office Politics

People talk about office politics because it is instrumental in determining whether you succeed long-term in an organization. Unfortunately, it is often a black box. Many people do not fully understand how office politics work and often feel helpless, particularly when things do not go their way. Office politics is an inextricable part of one's experience in an organization and is critically important to understand, but is so often misinterpreted or ignored, in the hope that it will disappear. However, as long as there are people involved, there will be politics.

Workplaces are an amalgam of people - those who want to get ahead, those who want to get along, those with tremendous intellect and drive, and those who merely want to skate. Office politics exists in all workplaces, whether there are thousands of employees or only one. It is human nature that most want to get ahead in the workplace, especially in organizations filled with large numbers of bright, driven people. Office politics is really a derivative of the social contract.

People often mistakenly give up the control they have on their professional path by chalking up whatever happens to them to office politics, rather than owning the situation and taking responsibility for what they can meaningfully change. There will always be certain things we cannot fix in our lives - and our working environment is no exception. However, we should not throw the baby out with the bathwater by completely relinquishing the control we do have.

Another misperception is that you can rely solely on what people say and do in trying to figure out the politics in your workplace. There are other dimensions - one's attitude, motivations and personal agenda - that are essential to recognize and figure out with those around you. You need to take a step back and understand what people say and do in the context of how they approach work so that you can better predict what they are going to do in any given situation, as well as where alliances lie and how certain situations are likely to play out. The predictability factor is critical in determining how you should best react, if at all, to any given situation. Office politics is not all about manipulation and backstabbing, nor do you have to play dirty to get ahead.

There are many lessons to keep in mind when it comes to managing how you engage in, or steer clear of, office politics. First, be realistic about whether the politics as they exist in your workplace is something you can successfully navigate and whether you can be happy and fulfilled at work. Second, you need to acknowledge the games people play. Things are not always what they appear to be; be cautious about what you believe, particularly when the information that comes to you is hearsay. Understand there is usually a spin put on everything, either intentionally or unintentionally.

This segues into another lesson learned - be careful what you say and do. You can be the straightest shooter there is, but if the people around you want to create drama, they may take something you say or do which is very straightforward and innocuous and spin and manipulate it to serve their purposes. That is why it is really important to have at least one person at work whom you can completely trust, and who completely trusts you, so that you can share information and help each other navigate the politics. It is always good to have someone who can help you think through what is happening and how to handle certain people and situations, and help ensure things do not come back to bite you.

David explains, *"During law school, my father, also a lawyer, taught me what I consider the essence of office politics: A little bit of brown-nosing never hurt anyone; too much will kill you."*

Mastering Delegation

There are only 24 hours in a day. Delegation enables you to get more done in less time when tasks are broken down into various pieces and done in parallel. Having people you can delegate to creates leverage, which is essential to staffing matters in an economical way, especially in an era where we must do more with less. It also helps ensure team members are focused. For those tasks that have already been mastered by certain co-workers, you should look for ways to involve other team members who can benefit from receiving cross-training on those tasks. Delegation is critical because no one person can do or know it all. It is important for efficiency, economy, training and creativity.

Delegation is a dynamic, not a static, concept. Over time, the best delegation evolves as people's skillsets grow. It takes into account how people are learning, developing and mastering various skills. It is important to strike a delicate balance of delegating the right amount and the right types of tasks to the right people. This means mastering the art of breaking projects into smaller pieces, knowing the resources available to you and their respective skills, and project managing each to ensure timely, effective completion. You must also consider what pieces of a project you will do yourself, whether you are growing through the process and giving yourself an opportunity to shine as well. Making the decision not to delegate at all, or to delegate less than you should, particularly in a professional services environment, is not what clients want. It is taking the easy way out and it is self-limiting behavior. Delegating too much can have its own problems, including taking significant risks with the quality of the product and losing control of a project. Through effective delegation, you learn what colleagues can do well and where they excel.

We often think delegating is too difficult and that it is easier to do things ourselves. Successful delegation of certain work is essential to our own successful performance. The key is being able to delegate to the right people who will get the job done well.

If you are in a situation where you are unable to delegate as much as you would like you should consider your options in terms of getting the work done that you have. This involves taking inventory of projects, what the deadlines are, how long they will take to complete, what you can reasonably expect your schedule to look like, what your other daily obligations will be and what juggling will look like. If you are in-house, you may be able to send some projects to outside counsel or, if you are part of a legal department, see if others can lend a hand with at least some of the work. If you are in a law firm, think of how to get both immediate and longer-term help, as the one-person-band model does not generally work in the long run.

Delegation is not just pushing work down to a direct report or someone more junior than you. It is a form of teamwork. Delegation often means relying on your non-lawyer business colleagues to help with work, which helps support the business as a whole.

Be Focused

Being focused is one of the key ingredients to performing at an optimal level. It makes you more effective since you are able to concentrate on thinking through issues and projects much more clearly and comprehensively. Focus also enables you to get into the flow more often and more seamlessly, which gives you the ability to have more frequent "aha" moments and to push the boundaries of your creativity. It also makes you more efficient at the various tasks you perform so that you are able to handle a greater volume of work over a shorter period of time. All of these factors contribute to enhancing your performance, which will ultimately help you to differentiate yourself in the marketplace.

Focus also enables you to drown out the noise of outside distractions, enabling you to maintain your train of thought and, quite simply, to get your work done. Focus enhances delivery of good client service. More than just focusing on paperwork, the concept includes focusing on the person you are with. Whether that person is your boss or your client, they will have a much better experience and appreciation for you and for the interaction as a result of you giving them your full attention.

When you are distracted by things going on around you rather than concentrating on what is in front of you, it can be tough to focus. It is easy to become scattered, which often happens when you are not completely clear on what is truly important to you and then developing your list of priorities based on those things. If you are spread too thin, or overtired and overly stressed, it can have a paralyzing effect. It is also tough when your work environment and habits are not conducive to developing and maintaining your focus. It is like having a finely tuned instrument or a well-developed muscle - it requires a significant commitment and determination to concentrate on the present moment, to the exclusion of everything else.

There are so many distractions during the workday. Days are filled with the telephone ringing, clients walking into your office, a constant barrage of emails - all of which are raising new questions and issues across a broad spectrum of substantive areas and most assuredly disrupting your intended schedule or agenda for the day. This can be quite jarring to your ability to focus. However, this explains why focus is so important, especially the ability to focus quickly on each new issue while pivoting from one person to another, one matter to another, one substantive area to another.

There is a certain mindfulness that is necessary in order to maintain your focus, particularly over a sustained period of time. The trick is to figure out how to get yourself to that place. Christina explains, *"I learned how to meditate a number of years ago and have found that it helps me to quiet my mind and get more in touch with my intuitive side. This helps to create a sense of inner calm and peace within so that I can stay more focused on what I am doing and remove the clutter of my mind so that I can perform to my full potential."*

It is also critical to develop a work style and environment that enables you to concentrate on what is in front of you. Whether it is turning off your phone and email for a while and closing your door, or taking a walk to clear your mind before jumping into a project, you need to develop ways that help you minimize distractions. These methods will vary from person to person. David explains, *"One technique I use is working to music; I actually find its absence distracting. I meditate every morning before leaving for work and I recommend taking breaks once in a while to clear your head, even if you just take a few seconds to close your eyes, take a couple of deep breaths and center yourself."* You might also try starting your day by clearing several smaller tasks off your to-do list so they do not nag you while you are trying to focus on a longer or more difficult task. If you need to focus for a long period of time on a single project such as writing a brief, try a change of scenery - working from a coffee shop, library, a conference room instead of your office or a different room in your house.

Humility

We often hear about humility, whether we are discussing human interactions in the context of business or world relations. It is a rather elusive virtue often in short supply, yet it is essential in our ability to take meaningful steps forward in many areas of our lives. Merriam-Webster's Dictionary defines "humility" as *"freedom from pride or arrogance."* Although it seems simple enough, it is exceedingly rare to see true humility in action. As one of the core emotional intelligence attributes, it is a key component in both transforming our organizations and in bettering ourselves as professionals.

So, what does humility look like? It means we put others before ourselves and strive to get beyond the surface in our communications in an effort to connect with other people in a more thoughtful, meaningful way. It is appreciating the importance of hearing other's points of view, thereby creating an environment conducive to sharing viewpoints, one where everyone feels like they are truly being heard. Listening plays an essential part in the success of this dynamic, and true collaboration is a byproduct of the process. It is creating a sense of "we," not just "me" and "you."

Humility is also understanding that we do not know everything there is to know, and that others are able to contribute just as much, if not more, than we can to a particular situation. It also means that we are not always prioritizing ourselves, our wants and desires. Instead, our attention is consistently focused on the needs, wisdom and contributions of others and what is best for the collective whole.

With humility, we recognize that we are not perfect, and we make a concerted effort to conduct ourselves in alignment with that knowledge. It means that we have come to terms with that aspect of ourselves, and it is a willingness to acknowledge our shortcomings to others. There are many lessons to be gleaned through the process of making mistakes, and it is through this imperfection that we experience a sense of vulnerability. By being able to convey this sentiment to others, we have an ability to relate to them and to understand different sides to issues and various points of view.

This, in turn, makes us more effective in our interpersonal communications in the long run, since we project a sense of accessibility, approachability and camaraderie that is essential in successful relationship building and decision-making. We cannot overestimate the importance of humility in our client relationships, and it is a critical element in effective client service. Our clients look to us as wise and knowledgeable counselors in our respective practice areas and expect us to effortlessly demonstrate that they chose wisely when retaining us. Whether they express it or not, they also expect us to strike that extremely delicate balance between consistently demonstrating our quiet confidence and displaying a healthy dose of humility.

While clients do not set out to hire wimpy lawyers, they most certainly do not want to be subjected to needless arrogance. It is our responsibility to be the very best practitioners we can be, and to believe in ourselves and in our ability to do our jobs effectively. At the same time, we must carefully modulate our behavior and attitude appropriately and make sure that our priorities lie first and foremost with our clients, rather than ourselves. When interacting with them, we should always ask ourselves if we are listening to what they are saying and reacting accordingly, rather than merely telling them what we want them to hear and what makes us feel good about our own expertise. True humility means a lot less talking and a lot more listening.

Humility is also an extremely important component of effective leadership. The best leaders intuitively understand there are myriad ways to achieve success, and it is often a product of synthesizing the thoughts and ideas of those whom they lead, rather than any independent epiphany the leader may experience. Projecting humility is a critical part of engendering the type of dialogue and sharing of ideas necessary to arrive at a desired result. Having that likeability factor and being able to instill confidence in others through empathy inspires others to act and are the hallmarks of a truly effective leader.

Ultimately, humility is a true selfless act, not a weakness by any means. In fact, it takes a great amount of strength and resolve to consistently demonstrate humility, both professionally and personally. And just as it is abundantly clear when we are seeing humility in action, it is likewise patently obvious when it is absent. As CS Lewis so wisely stated, *"Humility is not thinking less of yourself, but it's thinking about yourself less."*

Likeability

The analysis seems simple enough - if people like you, you will be happy and successful. But if it were that easy, then why isn't everyone doing it? The likeability factor - sometimes referred to as the LQ, for likeability quotient - remains an elusive concept. There is often an inherent tension and fundamental misunderstanding between the reality and fiction of what makes us likeable, what we should do to be more likeable and whether it is even important. And while we may believe we have an intuitive sense of all of these things, we are often shallow and misguided in our notions.

It is only in the past few years that we have even begun a meaningful conversation about likeability and its effect on our happiness and success. The simple fact is that we cannot have a robust workforce that will effectively perform over the short- and long-term if mutual admiration and collegiality do not exist in our workplace. We cannot effectively create client service teams if our colleagues who are essential to those relationships do not like us and want to help. Given that our professional world now consists of a waning demand for many types of legal services, clients have a multitude of great lawyers to choose from, and they simply will not work with us if they do not like and respect.

So, what does it mean to be likeable? It means we can readily relate to others, and vice versa. We do so by establishing common ground in relationships quickly and easily. We are thoughtful, engaging and focus on those with whom we are interacting in the moment, rather than allowing ourselves to become distracted and multitasking our way through a situation. We effectively empathize and see clearly the lens through which others view the world. We understand others' points of view, demonstrate that we truly hear what people are saying and act in accordance with that understanding. We meaningfully convey that we sense both the good and the bad that others feel and tailor our approach appropriately to the situation at hand and offer our assistance.

We are also authentic and genuine in our communications and create alignment between what we say and what we do. We bring a certain level of excitement to our professional and personal circles because of the passion we bring to all that we do, and that sentiment is contagious. Those around us feel like they have a strong sense of who we are and what we stand for and enjoy being with us. Indeed, trustworthiness, credibility and predictability are all critical ingredients of being likeable.

There are a few underlying themes here. Our ability to connect with others is an essential element of the likeability factor. As part of that, we need to gain an understanding of what motivates and inspires other people. What are they hoping to achieve, and how can we help them get there? How can we adapt our approach so that what we say and do is most impactful for them? Connecting with others is inherently a two-way street, and we need to remember that it is not all about us. In fact, being likeable is very little about convincing others how great we are and is much more about our ability to understand the people around us.

In determining what makes others tick and uncovering the common ground we all share, we should make a concerted effort to consider different points of view and listen carefully to what others have to say. We also need to be thoughtful in how we respond. Our most powerful communications are strategic and well-timed. We should also be keenly aware of our strengths and weaknesses and brutally honest with ourselves about what we do well and what we need to work on. We must take a close look at ourselves and ensure we are attuned to what others really think of us. The impression we make is a combination of many factors, including our intellect, personality, appearance and demeanor. It is important to have a positive attitude and understand that it is a powerful force that more readily precipitates the desired results upon which our clients and organizations thrive.

We also need to regularly take stock of the nature and quality of our interactions with others. We should be attuned to how we feel during these encounters, both mentally and psychologically. We must listen to our body, and whether we feel settled and balanced, or uneasy. We can pick up on the energy of others and how they are feeling by paying close attention to both verbal and nonverbal social cues. Sometimes we need to step outside ourselves and actively seek this type of feedback from those around us whom we respect and trust. This may include working with executive coaches and other similar professionals.

In considering what it means to be likeable, it is also important to know what it does not mean. Likeability is not about winning a popularity contest, nor does it mean that we are pushovers. In our quest to be likeable, we must be authentic and comfortable in our own skin. We cannot be everything to everybody, and there will be times when others may not like us, no matter how hard we try. And that is okay. While we should be sincere in our efforts to understand others and in treating them as we would want to be treated, we also should not take ourselves too seriously. None of us is perfect, and just making a good-hearted effort to connect with others will often go a long way.

Gravitas

Likeability is an important component of the overall package we offer clients, and its close cousin is gravitas. It is often used interchangeably with words such as charisma and executive presence. The Oxford Dictionary defines gravitas as *"the quality of being serious and dignified in manner, often commanding respect and trust."* and, according to the Urban Dictionary, it is *"strength of character, self-esteem, confidence."* Wikipedia mentions that gravitas is one of the Roman virtues, along with Pietas, Dignitas and Virtus and that it *"conveys a certain substance or depth of personality."*

Notwithstanding the fact that it is defined in any number of ways, gravitas still remains a bit of a conundrum. Historically, the term has mainly been used in the political realm, but as it has become an increasingly mainstream concept, it is often applied in other contexts, including in the media and business world.

As with other things which defy a clear-cut explanation, you know it when you see it. People with gravitas exude success, have an air of authority and leadership and command respect. They are effective communicators, they garner credibility and convey a wisdom often attributable to both age and experience. They have a level of confidence which is readily perceived by others, yet without projecting a sense of arrogance. Those with gravitas are authentic and align what they say with how they think and what they do, which makes their communications with others much more powerful and impactful. They project selflessness as their way of being, rather than selfishness.

There are a number of different components to gravitas. First, there is a certain level of substantive knowledge, intellectual horsepower and focus which is critical in establishing gravitas. We are able to successfully leverage our strengths but also recognize the limits of what we know and understand what we do not know, which allows us to seek the assistance of others as needed. This serves the greater good and is key in maintaining our credibility. Our appearance and demeanor, which include how we look, dress and present ourselves in both formal and informal settings, are also important. There is a level of assertiveness and self-assuredness which goes hand in hand with gravitas, and these are inextricably linked with our posture, body language and level of engagement when interacting with others.

Maintaining eye contact, having a firm handshake, delivering effective presentations and projecting our voice when speaking are just a few of the many examples of how we exhibit gravitas. Being a great communicator is also an essential ingredient. This means that we are able to take our knowledge and insight and successfully and passionately convey them to others in an inspiring way. We wholeheartedly believe in what we say and say what we believe. We are persuasive and project confidence and composure in our oral and written communications. When we have a healthy dose of emotional intelligence, we have the tools to take these communications to an even higher level, since we are finely attuned to ourselves and others. We are keenly aware of our audience in any given situation and understand the various points of view.

We hear both what is said and unsaid and are able to read the room for clues and suggestions on how to make adjustments to our approach in real time. Maintaining a high-level of engagement in a situation is an important element of gravitas. Developing and maintaining gravitas takes a lot of hard work. There is an age-old debate about whether it is something we are born with. As with most things in life, there are those who seem to effortlessly demonstrate gravitas, whereas others have a more difficult time with it. Regardless of which camp you are in, everyone can take steps in developing and harnessing gravitas. Working with professionals such as executive coaches and soliciting honest, frank feedback from friends and colleagues about our personal effectiveness and our strengths and weaknesses can be effective tools in our development. We also need to recognize that gravitas is not about bowling others over with how great we are. Rather, it is in the process of meaningfully connecting and making a positive difference, and in being kind and generous in the service of others, that our true essence, our gravitas, shines through. Whether we are born with it or are cultivating it from scratch, we must always look for ways to improve ourselves and our skills.

Gravitas is not just for politicians, newscasters and the C-suite anymore. Indeed, it has become increasingly important for all professionals, and lawyers in particular. Having gravitas helps to inspire the trust, confidence and peace of mind of clients. Given the continued evolution of the legal and business landscapes, clients are always seeking meaningful differentiators among their various service providers. Gravitas is often part of that "secret sauce" in the recipe for effectiveness and success.

Listening

We hear it all the time - there are few talents in a lawyer's arsenal more important than being a good listener. Listening is an essential component of effective communication, both as attorneys and as human beings. As children, we are taught early on that if we listen to our parents and teachers, we will be successful. As adults, we often lose the wisdom of this powerful lesson. Although simple in concept, effective listening nevertheless remains an elusive skill and is often difficult to do well.

There is usually a confluence of factors which leads to communication challenges. First, we all see the world through our own set of experiences and predispositions, each of which acts as a filter in our interactions with others. Thus, when we listen to what someone is saying to us, there can be a huge gulf between what that person is actually saying and what we are hearing. Our ability to effectively listen is also shaped by our overall feelings about the message being delivered as well as the person delivering it, either positive or negative.

We also live in a world of perpetual distraction, often making meaningful communication difficult. We are incessantly bombarded with a wide array of stimuli - the calls, emails, texts and meeting requests we receive all day every day. In our zeal to quickly juggle these demands through the fine art of multitasking, this sensory overload makes it easy for us to lose the essence of any given exchange. It takes special effort on our part to ensure that we do not pay short shrift to others, particularly clients, in this process.

Most people prefer to talk rather than listen, especially lawyers. There is a common misperception that those who talk the most are inevitably the smartest in the room or should garner the most respect, which is simply not the case. Rather than always trying to figure out what to say next, we should prioritize focusing on what others are saying to us in the moment and processing that information. Listening does not display weakness; rather, it shows respect for another person and demonstrates a true interest in understanding their point of view.

Sometimes communication gaps occur when the person we are speaking with does not say what they really mean. This often happens when there is an underlying fear of how others will react to the message or when there is a larger agenda at work. The discerning listener can nevertheless capture the real message, being sensitized to what is not being said and other nonverbal clues.

With all these communication issues, how can we ensure that we listen effectively, especially with our clients?

First, focus on the speaker. Provide your full attention and do not multitask. If necessary, turn off your phone, email and other distractions, particularly in a face-to-face meeting. Think generally about the other person, what you know about them, how they view the world and where they are coming from with respect to the issue being discussed. Think about how their position as well as their prior experiences may color and shape what they are saying and how they say it. Also consider how you would feel if you were that person and what you would be saying if you were in their shoes.

Then pay close attention to what is being said. Do not just listen to the words; also listen for the tone of voice and cadence, as well as for pauses, when those pauses occur and other similar cues. Watch for the presence or absence of nonverbal body language, such as facial expressions and eye contact and for posture and gestures. These clues can tell you a lot about the general mood of the speaker and how they are feeling. Do they seem happy, sad, angry, impatient, frightened, overburdened, skeptical, aloof or otherwise? Is their sentiment something they are merely feeling in the moment or is it more of a general state?

As you are listening, also consider why the person is speaking with *you* about this topic. Sometimes the answer is immediately obvious, but not always. You need to determine what is being requested of you, if anything. Are you being asked to take some sort of action or to provide advice, or are they merely bending your ear or venting? Understand that the person may not come right out and ask for your assistance. If the purpose of the conversation is not immediately evident, ask yourself whether there are bigger issues at play and consider whether there are any other dots you need to connect. This includes figuring out who else is involved and what is at stake in this situation for all of the relevant players.

As you are engaged in discussion, be sure to react appropriately. You should not only provide cues that you are both understanding and processing what is being said, but also follow up with ideas and questions as appropriate. As the conversation winds down, consider what is most appropriate under the circumstances to ensure that the other person feels heard and understood. This can be anything from developing an action plan to offering an expression of support or just agreeing to pick up the conversation again soon.

Sound simple? It can be, if you are focused and understand just how essential effective listening is to being the consummate professional. Just remember that as lawyers, we cannot deliver what a client wants, needs, and expects if we do not hear what they are asking for.

Passion

Finding passion in one's career can be an elusive quest; the law is no exception. Indeed, many lawyers express long-term dissatisfaction with their jobs and seek their true passion elsewhere. In fact, they will often stop practicing law altogether and take the plunge to pursue other interests on a full-time basis. Why the endemic unhappiness? We have all heard countless times that the law is a "jealous mistress," all-consuming and an endless source of stress.

This myopic view is typically born of the adage that the grass is always greener on the other side and fails to recognize that every other profession has also become much more demanding and stressful. There is little, if any, indication that those demands will ever abate. So what can we do? Channel your focus and energy on making the most of your career here and now and change that which is within your control, accept what we cannot change and have the wisdom to know the difference.

Being a positive force in our profession is born of passion. Passion is a critical part of any successful and fulfilling path. It is what motivates and excites you. Passion fills you with energy and a positive attitude and enables you to work tirelessly. It is at the heart of finding satisfaction in what you do, both personally and professionally. Satisfaction breeds happiness and happiness breeds personal and professional success. It is difficult to find one without the others. Passion also makes you more powerful and effective with clients and potential clients. They are well-aware that passion translates into dedication and delivering results on their matters. It shines through in all that you do and separates you from your competitors. It enables you to focus, reason and problem-solve in a much more meaningful way. Clients both want and expect their lawyers to go through brick walls for them, and passion enables you to preserve and push through to the finish line, despite the toughest of challenges. Passion converts inaction to action, and results rely on action. Passion also provides a more impactful framework within which to both lead and mentor others. When you are passionate about what you do, others will want to be around you and follow your lead. There is a heightened level of engagement and excitement that you bring to the table. Your team will be more receptive to your suggestions, ideas and advice and will perform at a higher level.

When team members are focused on the same goals, it enables them to be much more successful in driving the desired results, both individually and collectively. In addition, when you are passionate about what you do, your mentoring is more likely to resonate with mentees. When you share your experiences with them, your passion is palpable, contagious and attractive, and they will want all of the excitement and motivation that they see in you. You will inspire them to take a closer look at themselves to evaluate their current circumstances and to determine where their own true passions lie. Everyone has a passion - it is just a matter of finding it.

Whether you are helping others find their passions or seeking your own, it can be a challenging endeavor. Passions rarely fall into one's lap, and finding them often involves hard work. In many ways, it is not all that different from dating and is a journey of hits and misses before you find what you are looking for. It is both an internal and external process, and while you must look outside yourself to determine what interests and motivates you, it is important to remember that passion is a state of mind and, in large part, comes from within.

As with finding a mate, if you are jaded and pessimistic, you will have a more difficult time, but if you are patient, positive and have an open mind, you are much more likely to be successful. There may be myriad reasons why you are unhappy today which have little, if anything, to do with lacking passion. Following your passion does not mean perpetual bliss, and just because a career or circumstance is imperfect does not mean that passion is lacking.

Finding your passion is an evolutionary process that can and should unfold over many years. As people change and grow, so do their passions. By frequently considering what inspires and motivates you, you can continue to mold and shape your personal and professional life. Tweaks, rather than monumental changes, will often be enough. Ultimately, you may be one of those individuals who finds that the law is not your true passion and you may instead decide that finding success and fulfillment means that you must follow a different path.

Effective Practice Management

Whether within a law firm or a law department, practice management means ensuring that the client always comes first. It means successfully getting clients, doing a stellar job on the work and proliferating those relationships, and making sure the right talent is in place to service the work and to grow the business and keep it moving forward. It also includes developing strong relationships with all business colleagues, appropriate business stakeholders, and other key players.

There are many key ingredients to successfully managing a practice. Substantive lawyering is what drives the engine - and if you and your team are not great lawyers first and foremost, it makes it very difficult to successfully build, grow and manage a practice. For that reason, having a strong talent management program is key - particularly for associates - so that they get substantive, real-time feedback and can learn how to be better lawyers. A critical part of the teaching needs to be about client service, which goes way beyond just getting the right legal answer. It includes knowing how to properly frame the advice and understanding client's expectations on deliverables and becoming their trusted advisor. The financial aspects of managing a practice are also crucial. This includes ensuring there is alignment between how clients define value and what a particular matter will end up costing them. As with every other business, bills need to be timely paid to keep the lights on, and metrics such as utilization, realization and profitability are regularly examined.

Practice management involves a lot of moving pieces, and you need to make sure they all fit together in a way that makes sense and creates a pathway for success. It takes a village to sustain and propel a practice forward, and everyone should be respected for the part they play. Furthermore, practices are not static - they are fluid and dynamic - which means that people's roles will morph and change over time, particularly as they gain new and different experiences. It is important to take a step back and evaluate the situation holistically on a regular basis so as to make periodic adjustments in response to these changes. And just as those around you will evolve over time, so will you - so you need to look in the mirror often and think about your own growth process and where it is leading you.

Being Proactive

Being proactive means being at least several steps ahead, and seeing around the corner, for your clients and yourself. It is understanding the current state of affairs and how they came to be and where the situation is likely to head, given the balls that are currently in motion. It is acting in response to that knowledge, and not just allowing things to happen through the ordinary course. Being proactive is often discussed in the context of preventing bad things from happening, but can also be viewed as optimizing the ultimate outcome of any given situation.

Being proactive manifests itself differently in different practices and organizations, but generally, as a lawyer means being out in front of matters, taking the lead, and not necessarily waiting for your client to ask the question. Take the initiative rather than waiting to react. Some things require reactivity, such as lawsuits. However, you can use those situations to be proactive, such as advising a client how to avoid similar situations in the future, or perhaps suggesting certain additional terms for contracts or revising processes and procedures.

From Christina's perspective:

"As a young attorney, I channeled my efforts toward doing the very best job on every assignment. I looked at projects on an individual basis. As I have gotten more seasoned, I think more holistically about clients, rather than on a matter-by-matter basis. I try to understand the currents driving my clients' businesses and their legal needs. I seek to be much more multidimensional in my thinking, and in developing my skillset and an understanding of the business of law and how global political and economic issues shape certain events and have ripple effects on all organizations. Thinking about the world and my clients in this way enables me to be a better predictor of what is coming down the pike and enables me to think, plan and react accordingly."

There are many ways that lawyers can improve their proactivity, beginning with thinking more thoroughly about more issues more often. This will enable you to better understand how events and circumstances are much more predictable and within your control than meets the eye. It is important to be a student of human nature, and understanding people's motivations and agendas is a significant part of that, since those things will often drive certain actions and failures to act which, in turn, lead to various outcomes. Critical thought and analysis coupled with a healthy dose of psychology will serve you well in your quest to be more proactive.

Sometimes, being proactive is as easy as cultivating relationships with your clients. Get to know them as human beings as well as businesspeople. In turn, they will feel comfortable and compelled to seek your advice and counsel. Knowing your clients and their needs opens the doors to learning what is important to them and to the business, as well as to providing advice and suggestions ahead of the curve, rather than waiting to react.

Professionalism

The concept of professionalism has expanded significantly, and the term is used to refer to many more facets of a lawyer's performance than in the past. It used to focus on ethics and ensuring that you do not run afoul of the rules of professional conduct. Now, it more broadly encompasses your actions, behavior and attitude toward those with whom you interact - everyone from opposing counsel to clients, colleagues and others you encounter. Professionalism also gets to the heart of what motivates you as an attorney, what your focus is and even your personal brand. It makes you stop and ask yourself what others who know you would say about you. Law is a profession whose duties and responsibilities are a 24/7 proposition and pervade one's entire life. You cannot compartmentalize it.

While the perception of it has changed, professionalism itself has not. It remains the hallmark of the best lawyers - those who conduct themselves honorably, ethically and honestly, treating others with civility, striving at all times to achieve justice, fairness and the best possible results within the bounds of the law. The attitude toward professionalism and the practice of law generally has changed, with a continuing decline in civility, such as litigation gone awry with the focus on procedural gamesmanship rather than resolving conflicts on the merits, in the best interest of the clients, as quickly as possible. Lawyers are officers of the court, whether one practices in court or not, and what we do, and how we conduct ourselves, reflects on the institution of justice. When we conduct ourselves professionally, it reflects positively and fosters trust in the law and respect for lawyers.

Lawyers are competitive by nature. In large part, this quality helps you overcome whatever obstacles you encounter in your quest to succeed. Being competitive can enhance one's performance, which in turn drives better results for clients. However, this is never an excuse for lacking professionalism. Your reputation and integrity are at stake when you do things that demonstrate a lack of professionalism. Furthermore, lawyers in particular have to worry about tarnishing their reputation. We are in a service business, and if you compromise your reputation, you jeopardize your ability to generate business and to otherwise succeed in your practice. We also have to abide by a code of ethics, and if we run afoul of those rules, our licenses are at stake. Balancing these interests can be done effectively by following the golden rule. If you are thinking about pursuing an approach that you would find inappropriate if done to you, it is a strong signal that you should not do it.

A lawyer's competitiveness should be informed by professionalism. Everyone wants to win, but winning at all costs may well be antiethical to professionalism, especially if you are motivated by personal factors. David explains, *"Years ago, I represented a client in an acrimonious commercial litigation matter. Leaving the courthouse following a long day in a mediation where I first met opposing counsel, I said to him, I think we could be friends if we met under different circumstances. Fast forward several years, we are now good friends and I have used him as outside counsel in other cases. We competed intensely in the courtroom and became friends outside of it.* " This is how you balance competitiveness and professionalism. There is nothing wrong with being competitive, but do so with honor.

To improve your professionalism, you need to stop and think about what you are doing, or not doing, before you do it, and think about the potential consequences a few steps down the road. If necessary, seek the advice of people whom you hold in high regard. You should also continue to develop yourself as a professional and as an individual and engage in activities that will help you learn and grow. Finally, you should do what you can to avoid being put into situations where your professionalism either can or will be compromised.

Most people become lawyers because they want to help others, so you have to remember that we are a service profession. Be of service to others first, and be genuine about it. Always treat others with respect and dignity. Allow others whom you hold in high regard to be a role model and then pay it forward. For example, when opposing counsel clearly has chosen the high road over other options, find a way to tell them that you recognize their choice and appreciate it. That acknowledgment can go a long way as that instance of professionalism gets paid forward again.

Project Management

Effective project management is key because clients demand it. We see it with the trend in our industry towards alternative fee arrangements and other mechanisms which are making billable hours more obsolete. Just as certain industries such as manufacturing have successfully used principles of project management for years, the legal profession and other service industries such as medicine, accounting and consulting have evolved in such a way that their projects are likewise being broken down into their constituent parts and analyzed closely to drive greater overall efficiencies. There are various elements that go into effectively managing a legal project, including bringing in the right mix of talent that is both efficient as well as cost-effective. This analysis can become quite complex and requires skill in predicting how long the project will take, by when certain tasks need to be completed and by whom. It is also necessary to have a good sense as to where the project may go off the rails along the way and to have contingency plans lined up.

In this era of increasing pressure to perform at the highest quality for the lowest possible cost, project management is essential to success and organizational longevity. It is important to enable lawyers to complete their work efficiently, expeditiously and thoroughly. David explains, *"As an in-house lawyer, I cannot plan or manage projects in a legal vacuum. I must work closely with my business teams to discern their needs and goals and to understand the nature, scope, extent, resources and timing of any given matter. All of this is critical to successfully supporting my business colleagues and my company."*

The discussion about project management has evolved from being a somewhat avant-garde concept in the context of a legal practice to an essential skill in the toolbox of every lawyer who is trying to effectively manage client matters. Christina explains, *"Years ago, I studied project management as part of my Industrial Engineering Degree and, at the time, many people thought that service businesses such as law were mutually exclusive from this type of discipline. Now, nothing could be further from the truth."* Effective project management is crucial to help ensure that a firm is providing its services in the most streamlined, cost-effective way while also making sure it is maintaining the necessary margins to make the work worthwhile for the firm to perform. The principles of project management are simple: planning, processes, people and power. In addition to doing the requisite planning to be able to map the necessary processes and the people who will help execute it, you also need to know where the authority/power lies for decision-making.

The methodology of project management tends to be the same regardless of the task at hand. It begins with carefully defining what you are trying to accomplish, both substantively as well as from a timing standpoint, and then reverse engineering the project from there. There are both hard and soft deadlines built in along the way, with contingency plans in case the necessary resources get delayed or are unavailable, or if the results the client was hoping for do not come to fruition. This is a process that many attorneys struggle with, so we recommend that you make a concerted effort to master the principles and techniques of project management in order to put them to effective use in your practice.

Sound Decision-Making

Decisions. We make them all the time - at work and at home. Sometimes they are easy, and sometimes they are hard. Where to go to dinner, where to go to school, where to live, where to work. Our lives are filled with decisions both big and small, and we are forever living the consequences of the choices we make. A fundamental paradox of decision-making is that we often do not fully appreciate that we are making a weighty decision in the moment we are making it. Indeed, we often spend more time on the rather irrelevant decisions than we do on the important ones. That is because of the inherently uncertain, fluctuating nature of the world. When it comes to matters of great consequence, we often need to react very quickly, and we typically do not have all the time and information we need to fully vet the issue before making a judgment call.

The book *The Greatest Business Decisions of All Time* by Verne Harnish and the editors of *Fortune* magazine is a provocative commentary on leadership and decision-making through the examination of 18 different business decisions that fundamentally changed the course of various organizations. Some of them even precipitated a profound shift in a particular industry and in the world. There are a few important lessons about making business decisions that emerge from those stories.

First, we must have a supportive team around us whose skills and talents are complementary and readily adaptable. Second, it is critical to acknowledge that we may not know the right answer in advance, and we may need to be in the moment and make a game-time decision. We must also understand that, as leaders, we are not always able to gather all the data we need to make a decision, and we often have to rely on others to do the necessary due diligence.

Attorneys are acutely aware of the fundamental dichotomy between legal and business decisions. It has traditionally been our responsibility to advise clients on the legal risks presented by various options, and it is generally the client's role to make the ultimate decision as to how to proceed, given the context of their business. Since time immemorial, we have been very reluctant to go beyond the four corners of legal analysis and have historically taken the view that we are either ill-equipped to make business decisions or that it simply is not our place to make them.

We must recognize that while on the surface this division of labor may exist, there is much more to this dynamic than meets the eye. There is always a business context within which legal decisions are made, and in order for us to do what we do and to do it well, we must understand and implement the fundamentals of sound decision-making, from both the legal and business perspectives. We must also demonstrate to our clients that we are able to seamlessly straddle both worlds and can see the issues at hand from all of the relevant angles. Whether we realize it or not, we as lawyers are constantly making business decisions. Whether we are deciding to take on a certain matter, go to a networking reception or send out a work document now or later, these are all business decisions in some shape or form. But we typically do not recognize these choices for what they are and underestimate their importance.

In those moments when we are fortunate enough to recognize that we are making a business decision of great significance, we must separate truth from fiction rather than seeing things the way we hope or wish them to be. We have to be clear about our identity and what our goals and aspirations are in the context of our values. We need to be realistic about seeing the issues and challenges presented by the outside world and what is changing around us. We then need to reconcile who we are with the realities of our environment and determine what we are best positioned to do and what that will look like. It is through striking this delicate balance among numerous competing factors that we are ultimately able to make the best business decisions for ourselves and our organizations, both in the short- and long-term. Our clients need to know that we have strong decision-making skills and a keen intuitive sense and are able to perform, regardless of whether we have weeks or seconds to analyze a problem. Through effectively wearing both hats, we can then become a trusted advisor and successfully navigate the business of law.

Each of us makes a wide array of decisions every day, some of which are small and some significant. While we try to put thought into every decision we make, it is the small decisions each day that will take a back seat to the bigger ones, particularly if time and resources are limited. Christina explains, *"There are several steps I take, particularly while making the more significant decisions. First, I start by acknowledging when I am about to make a decision of consequence - there is something about doing that which shifts my focus and thought process in a meaningful way. I then gather as many facts as possible so that I can fully understand the context and different angles to the issue at hand. I also try to connect with those who have a vested interest in the outcome and who may have had to make the same or similar decision in the past."* It is important to see as many different facets to an issue as possible, and to hear from those upon whom you will rely to both support and help implement the decision.

As lawyers, we reason by analogy and make decisions based on that. Some decisions are easy to make quickly, while some require more in-depth analysis and consideration. David explains, *"Exactly how I make decisions depends on the type of issue involved, and for the most part I draw upon the facts, my experience, judgment and knowledge of law and business. I gather as many facts as possible and try to consider all possible issues and angles. I will likely talk to others who have a stake in the outcome. Then I synthesize everything and make a decision. I do not use a formal decision tree and analytical tool, much to the chagrin of my engineer wife and brothers-in-law. Nevertheless, there is a logical process in my thinking."*

Arriving at the right decision requires striking a delicate balance among several factors - fact gathering, consensus building and going with your gut. Even if everything seems to generally check out, if you feel uneasy about a particular decision, your intuition may be telling you that further vetting or consideration of the issue is in order. There are some decisions that benefit from the input of a trusted advisor, someone with whom you can discuss tough decisions and not take it personally if they tell you something you may not like hearing.

The common thread in many decisions is letting go. This can be a very difficult thing to do, even though it is often what is best. Having faith that things generally work out the way they are supposed to can be helpful in navigating these challenging inflection points.

Taking Risks

Taking risks is a fundamental part of life. It pushes us to meaningfully learn, grow and adapt and enables society to progress. Risk poses an interesting paradox over time. In our youth, many of us are willing to take risks of all shapes and sizes, sometimes at potentially significant physical, emotional or financial expense. Some call it foolish, others call it having little to lose. Over time, we often experience a marked shift in our relationship with risk and how it fits into our lives. Most people become more risk averse as they get older. This is often attributed to the wisdom one gains over the years and life experiences that come with time. Many believe that the more successful they become, the more they have to lose and, as a result, they are more mindful of the potential consequences of taking risks. Fear of failure sets in and often quells one's desire to step outside the norm and try something different, whatever it may be.

Fear and risk-taking are often closely intertwined. While fear has its place and can effectively protect us from danger, we must also recognize when it lacks foundation and do our best to properly modulate it. For some, taking risks is just not part of their personality and they are risk averse by nature. Many of us lawyers fall into this category. Those characteristics which make us uniquely qualified to advise clients regarding risk mitigation inevitably push us to perform the same analysis for ourselves and often leads us to steer clear of risk. We cannot help it - it is simply part of our DNA.

We must constantly strive to effectively balance numerous competing factors in our lives. Risk-taking should be no exception. We need to effectively discern those risks which may be a stretch but are nevertheless worth taking - the calculated risks - and those which are not, and we must govern our actions accordingly.

We should be willing to make mistakes along the way or, to at least, expect that circumstances may not turn out exactly as we wanted. We need to understand that encountering the unexpected does not mean that the venture was not worth it. Ultimately, being successful does not mean we have never failed. Rather, it means having a life rich in texture as a result of myriad experiences which make us grow and enable us to enjoy its many facets without regret.

We also have to welcome the serendipity that manifests itself in our lives and the benefits - and risks - that are often presented as a result. Risk is usually wrapped into those unique opportunities which arise and which we are compelled to pursue. Life is full of surprises and has potential for great rewards. We just need to see and recognize this, be willing to stretch and step outside our comfort zone and not allow our fear to control the situation, or us. We must also understand that on the other side of risk and fear lies the potential for great reward.

From Christina's perspective:

"Risk has played an important role in my life. Many years ago, I was a college student studying manufacturing. I began pursuing my Master's Degree in Safety Engineering and had worked for two summers at Motorola and received an offer for full-time employment upon graduation. My mother had recently died and finances were a significant struggle for my family. I was paying for my own education and was looking forward to graduating from school and beginning my career as an engineer. The plan seemed perfect and much of its perfection was in its predictability - until I was accepted into law school. My head was saying I should defer starting law school for a year; work as an engineer and save money. But my heart and my intuition were telling me something different - that I should delay starting my engineering career, jump into the deep end and start law school.

There were a number of significant risks associated with this option - finances, job prospects and the big unknown of a legal career, as I was the first in my family to go to law school. Ultimately, after much consideration, I decided to go to law school straight out of college. While there were moments I felt truly overwhelmed and feared that I had made the wrong decision, or the right one at the wrong time, I now look back more than 30 years later and know that it was the right thing to do and do not regret my decision for a moment."

Being a Trusted Advisor

Being a trusted advisor means that you are a client's go-to person to discuss a wide array of issues, both within and outside of your practice area. You are a confidante, so that when concerns arise and decisions are being made, you are one of the first people who your client wants to consult. You are an invaluable partner and resource with a high level of credibility and trustworthiness. In addition to having the requisite book smarts and education, you also have a very practical wisdom that enables you to understand the overall context of an issue or problem from various angles. You are also caring and empathetic, and while you revel in your client's successes, you are also often up at night worrying about the matters which matter to them.

Trusted advisors have built a level of trust and confidence with clients so that they not only seek your advice but rely on you as their go-to consultant/advisor/sounding-board before they move forward on a particular project or decision. To be a trusted advisor means you are known for having particularly strong judgment, credibility and trustworthiness, and others come to you for advice and consultation as a result.

Everyone wants a trusted advisor, especially clients who are often called upon to make complex, multifaceted judgment calls at lightning speed. They appreciate being able to call upon lawyers with industry knowledge whom they trust implicitly and who can draw from a breadth of relevant personal and professional experience to assist in their decision-making process. Having this type of dynamic enables a more effective flow of information and allows for a greater level of candor and understanding which helps ensure optimal decision-making. Being able to develop and maintain a trusted advisor relationship is also significant in differentiating yourself from other lawyers in the marketplace.

Being a trusted advisor is one of the hallmarks of being a lawyer and is essential to one's success in the profession. Those with the reputation of being a trusted advisor enjoy the greatest career success - this could mean money, titles, personal satisfaction or fulfillment. Generally speaking, lawyers like to help people and to make a difference for others. Being a trusted advisor is emblematic of success in achieving those goals.

Becoming a trusted advisor requires skill, commitment and time. You have to be good at developing relationships with clients, and there is a certain level of rapport that is essential before a client will let you in. You must have an innate understanding of the client as a professional and as a person and what makes them tick. You have to have their best interest at heart and make their problems your own. No matter how challenging a situation may be, clients always have to find a solution which optimizes a number of competing interests - rarely will the answer *"it cannot be done"* work, so your suggestion needs to take this reality into account. It is also critically important to remember that all clients are people with strengths, weaknesses, fears, responsibilities and opinions of their own and that they are trying to do their best in any given situation. By being a strong sounding-board, you can create long-lasting relationships built on mutual admiration and respect.

There are many different paths, elements and traits to becoming a trusted advisor. You must possess strong judgment, ethics and morals. Gaining a depth of knowledge is critical, not simply about the relevant law but also about your client's business and the issues you are working on with them. It is also essential to know your client as a person. This is yet another example of where emotional intelligence comes into play and is so important. To become one's trusted advisor, you have to develop a close bond. This does not require friendship - that helps but is not required - but it does require developing a relationship built on mutual trust and respect. Impeccable honesty, judgment, credibility, reliability and authenticity are traits that enable one to become a trusted advisor for others.

Recommended Reading List

- *A Minute to Think*, by Juliet Funt

- *Built to Last*, by Jim Collins & Jerry I. Porras

- *Drive*, by Daniel H. Pink

- *Emotional Intelligence: Why It Can Matter More Than IQ*, by Daniel Goleman

- *Emotional Intelligence 2.0*, by Dr. Travis Bradberry & Dr. Jean Greaves

- *Feel Good Productivity*, by Ali Abdaal

- *Freakonomics*, by Steven D. Levitt & Stephen J. Dubner

- *From Strength to Strength*, by Arthur C. Brooks

- *Good to Great*, by Jim Collins

- *Leading in the Law with Emotional Intelligence: The Path to Becoming a Twenty-First-Century* **Leader**, by Rob Durr & Cliff Zimmerman

- *Memories, Dreams, Reflections*, by Carl Jung

- *Mirroring People*, by Marco Iacoboni

- *Moneyball*, by Michael Lewis

- *My Beloved World*, by Sonia Sotomayor

- *Outliers*, by Malcolm Gladwell

- *Quiet: The Power of Introverts in a World That Can't Stop Talking*, by Susan Cain

- *Revenge of the Tipping Point*, by Malcolm Gladwell

- *Start with Why*, by Simon Sinek

- *Steve Jobs*, by Walter Isaacson

- *Strategy and the Fat Smoker: Doing What's Obvious but Not Easy*, by David Maister

- *Super Freakonomics*, by Steven D. Levitt & Stephen J. Dubner

- *The Greatest Business Decisions of All Time*, by Verne Harnish

- *The Speed of Trust*, by Stephen M.R. Covey

- *The Tipping Point*, by Malcolm Gladwell

- *Where Good Ideas Come From: The Natural History of Innovation*, by Steven Johnson

ADDITIONAL RESOURCES

Be sure to check out the **Paradigm Shift Podcast** by scanning the QR code below or by searching on your favorite podcast streaming platform.

We welcome any thoughts, questions and feedback you may have regarding this or any of the other titles in the *Paradigm Shift Series.* Our contact information is available below. We would love to hear from you!

Christina L. Martini
christinamartini.paradigmshift@gmail.com

David G. Susler
davidsusler.paradigmshift@gmail.com

NOTES

NOTES

NOTES

NOTES

NOTES

NOTES

NOTES

NOTES

NOTES

NOTES

NOTES

NOTES

NOTES

NOTES

Notes

NOTES

NOTES

Notes

NOTES

NOTES

NOTES

NOTES

NOTES

NOTES

www.ingramcontent.com/pod-product-compliance
Lightning Source LLC
Chambersburg PA
CBHW040755220326
41597CB00029BA/4839